The Obvious Choice

OTHER BOOKS BY JONATHAN GOODMAN

Ignite the Fire: The Secrets to a
Successful Personal Training Career

Viralnomics: How to Get People
to Want to Talk About You

THE WEALTHY FIT PRO'S GUIDES
Book 1: Starting Your Career

Book 2: Online Training (with Alex Cartmill)

Book 3: Getting Clients and Referrals (with Mike Doehla)

TEXTBOOK
The Fundamentals of Online Training
(Available at www.theptdc.com/ota)

FOR CHILDREN
Adventure, Adventure Awaits for Us All
(with Alison Goodman)

The Obvious Choice

*Timeless Lessons
on Success, Profit, and
Finding Your Way*

Jonathan Goodman

HarperCollins
LEADERSHIP

AN IMPRINT OF HarperCollins

For Alison

My girl. You're smart, beautiful, caring, and kind.
You put everybody else first and attack life
with strength, with joy, and with poise.

I love when you smile that smile that's a real smile.
I love your playfulness, and, of course,
I love your legs that scream, "I squat."

Thank you for doing the hard work so that I get to play around
with businesses and muck around with words.

Let's never stop exploring together. I love you.

CONTENTS

Business Was Great, Once

One moment I was riding high, admired for what I'd built. The next moment, I was crying at my kitchen table, telling my general manager about his severance package on a video chat.

The story starts when I produced the first-ever course for online fitness training. We owned the market from 2013 to 2020. Days with $100,000-plus in sales were normal.

Then, in March 2020, the COVID-19 pandemic shut down the world. While others suffered, my business soared. Overnight, and for reasons outside of their control, every personal trainer needed to work online.

It's super freakin' weird to write this, but the onset of the pandemic was basically a four-leaf clover shoved up the proverbial butt of my business.

We stopped doing everything that made us successful and hired costly brand consultants who told us how to speak and data analytics experts who told us how to convert. Drowning in reports, spreadsheets, and project briefs, I lost my way.

When you lose yourself, you forget why you're doing what you're doing. You show up and you do the work, but then you get home at the end of the day with nothing accomplished.

Expenses exploded, sales flatlined. Business wasn't fun anymore. We were working so hard and spending so much money, and none of it was making a damn difference.

But none of that mattered, because, on July 23, 2021, I came home to find my son playing by himself.

"Mommy's sad," he said.

I walked upstairs to the bedroom. Alison was crying.

"I have cancer," she said.

We fell into each other's arms.

My business needed me. My family needed me. I didn't know what to do. All I knew was that I needed space. So, in September 2021, I fired everyone.

—

Cancer's unfair. I don't wish it on anybody. It does, however, have a habit of calling you out on your shit. Alison's diagnosis forced a fresh start. After we knew that she was going to be okay, it was time to build our business back up.

By this time, in addition to generating tens of millions of dollars in my own business, we had directly helped more than 65,000 individuals build and grow their own thing through our programs and coaching. This experience helped me develop and refine in very practical and specific terms what makes a person successful. When applying these lessons to myself, I began to realize that my own business did not need to be such a struggle.

While everybody else seemed to be distracted by shiny objects, the secret to avoid that, I'd learned, was to build a foundation on the stuff that worked before the internet existed—a devolution of sorts, back to a simpler time. To do less, but better. To look at modern marketing technology as an amplifier, not an ignitor. As fuel, not the fire.

Here's a few of the insights that I gained the freedom to apply:

- Creating content is an overrated way to build a business short-term, but an underrated way to learn and connect.
- What you do to get results doesn't matter to others. What matters to others is what they'll become as a result of what you do.
- Large audiences are inefficient for deepening relationships. Trust needs touch. It is easier, faster, and more profitable to be famous to the family than it is to be famous on the internet.
- A product or service must be either free or expensive. Combine the two for explosive growth. Avoid the middle.
- Endlessly searching for the "best" way to do something is a surefire way to fail. Good enough, repeatedly, is how to get great.
- We often don't have a problem with authenticity. We have a problem trusting that our authentic self is enough.
- Our social media bubble represents maybe 0.01 percent of what goes on in the world that affects us and likely closer to 0.0000001 percent of what goes on in the world at large.
- In our world, we think that we know what matters. However, others don't live in our world, they live in theirs.

The truth of these insights (and others you'll read about) is self-evident and can be validated by your own experience as well as common sense. As you read this book, you may wonder how anybody succeeds in business without them.

It took some time to build back up, but the results have been remarkable. Revenue increased 300 percent with multimillion-dollar profitability and one-fifth of the staff.

As I began sharing these insights along with implementation strategies and case studies with my mentorship clients and with listeners on my podcast—also called *The Obvious Choice*—their lives and businesses were also enriched.

Take Benjamin, for example. He'd just gotten engaged and decided it was time to grow his side gig to make some extra cash to buy a home. Before we met, he had just started a page on social media and had been posting content for a month.

His hope was that it would somehow magically lead to awareness, which would in turn somehow magically lead to customers. "A part of me knew that what I was doing on social media didn't make sense, but I didn't know another way," he said.

I call this the Underpants Gnomes Problem, prompted by a famous episode of *South Park*. The gnomes steal underpants and expect profit, but miss the middle step of how one thing leads to the other. You'll read more about it in Chapter 6, "Figure Out What Game You're Playing Online."

Instead of trying to impress people he'd never met, Benjamin followed the five-step Human Optimized Marketing System you'll read about in Chapter 11, "Become Famous to the Family." He made his first sale that day.

The ugly truth is that social media is a gloriously inefficient way to build a business. Consider it a savings account, an investment into long-term career capital. Make deposits with extra time and money. Hope it kicks off interest, but don't depend on it for short-term returns. Much more on this, and a four-stage, content-creation framework in Chapter 14, "Social Media Is Not Enough."

———

Instead of going for the biggest possible audience, those who understand the Obvious Choice know precisely who they're for (and not for), and they don't fall into the trap of trying to win the internet. They have a clear vision that allows them to get more benefit with less effort from their marketing while simultaneously removing all comparison to others. The result is a simpler and more reliable approach with higher profitability in less time and with less stress.

Admittedly, there's a trade-off. The Obvious Choice might not become famous, celebrated in the media, or heralded as an against-all-odds, billion-dollar, unicorn success story.

For those who follow these principles, three to five million dollars in annual profit is the limit of what can be achieved with reliability, sustainability, and expectancy while maintaining a high quality of life. Though more is possible, it shouldn't be expected.

The reason for this limit is simple: at a certain point, more risk and more sacrifice are required to reach increasingly higher levels of income. Some people decide to accept this trade-off in exchange for a potentially larger windfall in the future. That's fine. Nobody's crazy. You won't find those stories celebrated here, however. Instead, we'll focus on the strategies and principles with the highest odds of success.

———

In 1982, John Naisbitt wrote in *Megatrends*, "The more high technology around us, the more the need for human touch." He was right back then. He's right today. *The Obvious Choice* is about human connection, not technological domination.

This book is about the business that happens behind closed doors.

More than 90 percent of sales are "silent" in that they still happen through a combination of trust and word-of-mouth referrals. There's undue attention placed on the remaining 10 percent—the scraps—because they're easy to track, measure, and analyze.

By the time a sale can be measured, all the Obvious Choices have already been hired.

For every eighteen-year-old on social media who thinks they need a big following just to get a few customers, there are a hundred silent business owners quietly earning more money with less effort. If you're having trouble finding your way, the problem isn't you. The problem is what you've been made to believe it takes to succeed.

Building a business and becoming an online entertainer are different games people play. Neither's better or worse, but they have different time horizons, rules of engagement, odds of success, and reward mechanisms. Problems arise when you conflate the two—playing by the rules of one and desiring the rewards of the other.

You don't have to dance on the internet to succeed. If you want to dance, go for it. Clean up those Pumas. Get out there. Have fun. I'll buff up my 3-Stripe Adidas and join you.

All I'm saying is that you don't *have* to perform to the anonymous masses just to make a few sales. You never did, and you'll never need to. There's always been a faster, easier, and more reliable path to success, and there always will be.

—

One thing I've found to be true is that you spend years learning new stuff only to realize that there's maybe like ten to twenty big ideas that impact you. I've also realized that most business books contain one big idea stretched out. As a result, readers get the point and give up on it.

This book is different. It contains fifteen big ideas. They all revolve around a common theme, but can also be read independently of one another.

You might not connect with every idea. I'd be surprised if you did. We tend to zero in on immediate needs or frustrations. If you're reading something that isn't jiving with you, you have my permission to skip it and move on to the next chapter.

My hope is that the ideas you do connect with will help you make more money, help more people, and have more freedom.

Let's go.

PART 1

A Few Not-So-Obvious Truths

—

CHAPTER 1

When Ambition Results in Recklessness

Broken Clocks — The Bug
Called "You" — Removing Recklessness

The process of becoming the Obvious Choice begins with subtraction, not addition.

When we know what we want, we can clarify what we don't want. And even painful decisions, though not easy, become simple.

It's likely you're already doing many of the right things, but they're being suffocated under a carpet of chaotic ambition.

—

I penciled in the last bubble and raised my hand.

"Are you done?" the woman asked.

I looked up at her.

"Yeah, I guess I am," I said.

Then I walked out of the university auditorium for the last time, utterly unaware and unprepared for the real world.

Maybe you've just finished college or maybe you decided not to go. Maybe you've been in the working world for a while. Or maybe you've done some great things already and had some success, either as an employee or entrepreneur. Regardless of where you're at, we all remember the moment when we had a challenging realization:

Our world isn't a paint-by-numbers kit.

As young people, we're told what to do, how to think, and when and where to show up. Success is simple to understand: good grades are good, and bad grades are bad.

Then we grow up and realize that life isn't best lived by the kind of guy who only eats cheese in single slices. The rules aren't black and white. More so, grayish.

Should you try to get rich? Maybe.

How rich? I don't know.

Will getting rich make you happy? Probably not.

What will? I don't know that either.

For the ambitious, this ambiguity is hard to reconcile.

—

Broken Clocks

People tell you that ambition is the key to achieving your goals.

Ambition—be *ambitious*.

You hear it all the time. Ambition fuels passion. Creates a purpose in life. "Where there's no ambition, there's no success," they say.

What those same people don't tell you is that ambition left unchecked results in recklessness. It's comparison. It's never thinking that you're enough. It's living inside your own fantasy.

Your ambition might be the very thing holding you back from accomplishment.

Now, more than ever, our culture fans the flames of chaotic ambition. We can follow and interact with our idols on social media, read any one of the 11,000 new books published every day, or add to the 226 million podcast episodes downloaded weekly. It's a fire hose of inspiration and education like never before. More often than not, what you're left with isn't confidence in your process but delusion.

Everywhere you look, somebody is achieving something better than you, faster than you, and has figured out something you *need* to know, or else (or else what?).

All of this results in constant disappointment because, if you're not careful, your expectations will rise faster than your results, no matter how much you've accomplished.

Whenever I think about how constant comparison to others' perceived success online is affecting my satisfaction, fulfillment, and well-being, I laugh the laugh human males tend to laugh when they want to hide emotion.

——

Jason had a great business. It was simple. It was profitable. And he did a good job. He wasn't famous on the internet but had built a local reputation. Old-school stuff.

One day his friend Maggie suggested he build an app to scale. She had good intentions. Maggie said her friend Jennifer has one and it seems to be going well.

Jason follows Matthew on Instagram. Matthew's always posting pictures with his girlfriend, traveling to exotic places and promoting his app.

"Does anybody know any app developers?" Jason posts in an online industry group one night. Recommendations are made. Sales calls are performed. Jason commits to a few thousand dollars, which quickly turns into a few more thousand dollars.

His app is ready. He prices it at $20 a month. Why $20? That's what others do.

A few friends buy to support him. Then he has to find more customers but doesn't know how. He's never paid for ads or used social media to get customers before.

Unknowingly, Jason's gone from a simple business model where he needs a few customers paying him a lot to a complicated one that needs a lot of customers to pay him a little. He's learning the hardest-to-learn law of business: just because you build it doesn't mean they will come.

"Does anybody use a good social media growth agency?" Jason posts in the same group. Again, recommendations are made. Sales calls are performed. Jason commits to a few thousand dollars more.

Six months have passed. Jason's burned out. His local business is suffering. He's been focused on the app. It's time to renew his contract with the development company. He's delaying the decision by doom-scrolling Instagram when a post from Matthew appears in the feed. "I'm shutting down my app," it says.

———

Good business models get traded for bad ones. The ill-fated allure of seeking shortcuts is simply too tempting for many.

Inevitably, modern tactics and attention-grabbing high-risers flame out like Icarus too close to the sun, only to be replaced by another, to whom we then compare ourselves. The cycle repeats.

Leveraging technology to scale isn't a bad thing. It obviously can work. But it works less often, less reliably, takes longer, and requires more effort than you think. There's no free lunch. For many of us, the oldest business models are still the best business models.

It's true that there's always a way to cheat the system, but things always change with gimmicks. If you're constantly searching for a success hack, you might stumble upon one. Even a broken clock is right twice a day.

Chaotically ambitious individuals who chase fads rarely win out over an extended period. And yet, missing out on the short-term can be a hard pill to swallow, especially when others' success seems sudden and extreme.

Personal and professional success isn't the result of brilliance; it's the reward you get for being consistently not stupid longer than the other guy. For finding your way in a world determined for you to lose it.

—

The Bug Called "You"

The search shouldn't be for what works best. Rather, how to be your best self.

No one will understand you. It isn't ultimately that important.

What's important is that you understand you.

We're all encoded differently. Your encoding goes beyond what you're good at. It's what you seem to naturally "get."

This isn't a better or worse thing. Some of us are made out to become professionals like lawyers, doctors, or accountants. Others are encoded to be tradespeople, entrepreneurs, or creatives. That doesn't make anybody smarter or stupider. Different people are different.

When an entire world that doesn't know you is determined to tell you what to do, how to think, and who to become, the first step is to turn the microscope around.

Easier said than done.

Before he sold millions of copies of *Good to Great*, the business author Jim Collins's Stanford professor Rochelle Myers inspired him to study himself in much the same way that a scientist would study a bug, to imagine *he* was the bug—the bug called "you"—by keeping a Bug Book.[1]

It's hard to separate our actions from our motivations. Our feelings from our insecurities. Our facts from our biases. But scientists . . . scientists view the world as dispassionate and objective outsiders. Scientists don't judge what they study. Scientists merely observe.

Examination of yourself like what I'm about to describe might seem weird. At its core, this is a journaling exercise. And if you're not a journal person, don't worry, neither am I.

Set an alarm to alert you five times a day for a week. When the alarm goes off, give yourself a score from minus-2 to plus-2 in 0.5 increments. Minus-2 means you're feeling awful. Plus-2 means you're feeling amazing.

Beside your score, add anything meaningful from what you're doing, to who you're with, to what you ate, and anything else. Make your observation objective. Don't add commentary or assessment. Give yourself a score. Add additional observations. And close the book.

You can download a Bug Book worksheet to better study yourself at www.JonathanGoodman.com/Bug.

You can create your own Bug Book by dividing a page into four columns for the date, time, score, and observation. When your alarm

Date	Time	Score	Observation
Nov 7	9 am	+ 1.5	Biking Calvin to school with entire family.
	12:30 pm	+ 2	Focused writing, two-hour block.
	1:30 pm	- 0.5	Lunch. Not relaxing. Eating with one hand, phone in the other.
	4 pm	- 1.5	Brain fog. unfocused.
	8 pm	- 2	Got caught in cycle of watching dumb internet videos while family is upstairs. Snuck too many post-dinner cookies.

goes off, fill in each column. When collecting your data, only write observations. Resist the urge to comment, analyze, or react.

At the end of the week, review all your minus-1s and minus-2s in addition to your plus-1s and plus-2s. Note any patterns. Then, write third-person observation statements.

Here are a few of mine from over the years:

- "The bug Jon felt energized when he woke up at 5am on a Saturday morning to write his book."

- "The bug Jon felt brain fog when he scheduled two meetings on video back-to-back without a break."

- "The bug Jon felt alert for his next call when he scheduled a fifteen-minute break in between video meetings to go for a short walk."

- "When the bug Jon reads fiction for fun, the world makes sense and moves at a more manageable pace."

- "The bug Jon thinks Starbucks's made-up language is ridiculous and still asks for a medium when ordering a coffee because that's the proper word to use when describing the size of drink that he wants."

- "The bug Jon likes creating content, but the acts of formatting and publishing to social media sap his energy and give him brain fog."

Revisit this process at least every six months, or as often as necessary if you feel you're losing your way. Many find it useful as an ongoing awareness exercise. I do.

———

Removing Recklessness

Just one thing keeps chaotic ambition going—anxiety. Keeping busy soothes our fear. Doing something saves us from the hard work of figuring out whether what we're doing is making any damn difference.

Too often we find ourselves driven, yet tired. Motivated, yet anxious. Hardworking, yet frustrated and burned out. So much of what we do when we're working hard simply doesn't matter; it's a reformative effect of our fast-paced, social-media-driven environment, the crushing pressure of ambition and competitiveness.

Nobody wants to be this way any more than they wanted to sit at the table at the back of the cafeteria on the first day of high school; it's just something we've somehow all collectively accepted as how things are.

Recklessness, however, isn't a necessary or inevitable condition of life; we chose it, if only by our acquiescence to it. When we remove chaos, we're left with what's real. Whereas chaos lays waste to our efforts, true ambition is a powerful ally.

Chaotic ambition is reactive, comparative, and rushed. It leads to frustration and burnout.

True ambition is proactive, thoughtful, and strategic. It allows for calculated risk and provides the energy and direction necessary for achievement.

It has become very easy these days to work very hard on the wrong things.

The secret to doing less and having more is to know yourself, and how you work, better. That's why the first step to becoming the Obvious Choice is to focus inward—to study yourself as an objective and dispassionate outsider—like a scientist, a scientist studying a bug.

Next, let's talk about why credentials don't matter much (and what does).

CHAPTER 2

Trust in You > Your Credentials

The Synagogue's Board — It Hertz — Your World ≠ Their World — The Dude — Finding Perfect Customers with the Marble Method — Beating Michael Jordan

In our world, we know what makes us reputable. We've put in the work to earn the credentials.

Others don't live in our world, though; they live in theirs.

While the same knowledge and experience that make you reputable might help you deliver a great product or service, they won't help you become the Obvious Choice.

Humans don't buy things as a result of good decisions made with complete evidence. Instead, we trick ourselves into thinking that we're making educated decisions. It's embarrassing. You won't want to admit it. I don't.

The problem isn't that we don't want to make a smart purchase; it's that there's too much to know.

How can you, or anybody who buys from you, be expected to gauge quality in a field they don't understand?

I hope you never have to find a cancer doctor. It's not the type of thing you're ever prepared for. Here's the wildly irresponsible way we found ours.

I called a doctor friend and asked for a referral to an otolaryngologist (ear, nose, and throat specialist). He gave us the name of Dr. E., saying, "I've heard he's the best." We then worked tirelessly to get accepted by Dr. E. Nobody else mattered—it *had* to be Dr. E.

Here's a few things I ignored at the time:

1. Our friend didn't know anybody Dr. E. had treated.
2. Our friend's an addiction psychiatrist.
3. Our friend's never had cancer.
4. We never checked Dr. E.'s references.
5. We never looked into Dr. E's education.
6. We didn't check if Dr. E. had ever published original research.

All the things Dr. E. probably values (schooling, credentials, continued education, past successes, and published papers) were things we ignored when deciding to hire him. He had a bunch of letters behind his name. They were probably important. To me, they were gobbledygook, meaningless alphabet soup.

We trust the word of a friend, neighbor, or coworker more than that of a stranger—even if the friend knows nothing and the stranger is a bona fide expert.

None of this, of course, changes the fact that there are 49 million kangaroos in Australia and 3.5 million people in Uruguay, which means if the kangaroos were to invade Uruguay, each person would have to fight fourteen kangaroos. But I digress.

Dr. E. ended up being a good doctor. My wife got treatment. She's healthy. It's gone.

Fuck cancer.

Still, I can't help but think that if this was how I chose a professional to help in the most extreme of circumstances, how bad must my day-to-day decision-making process be?

I consider myself well-educated. I mean, geez, I write books that smart people like you read that only occasionally include sexual innuendo, bad nineties references, and jokes about fictional characters making out with their sisters.

And yet, even though I'm a guy who writes books about this stuff, my family's reasons for hiring a doctor to treat my wife's cancer were objectively bad.

Trust transcends expertise. It's more important than your credentials and can be created through any combination of three factors:

1. Community—proximity, association, or affiliation

2. Specificity—suited uniquely

3. Familiarity—repeated exposure

Let's now look at an example of a financial advisor, TV salesman, and a dude selling meat door-to-door who all became the Obvious Choice by building trust.

—

The Synagogue's Board

I've sent Ted Rechtshaffen millions of dollars.

He's our financial advisor—a coach and strategist responsible for my family's wealth. In fees alone, I pay him tens of thousands of dollars a year.

How'd I choose him?

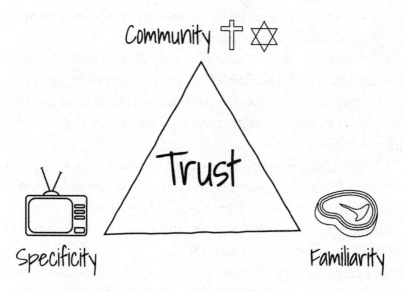

He sits on the board of our synagogue—a synagogue that I haven't attended for more than twenty years.

Affinity to you results from a shared background, experience, philosophy, or membership in an organization. **Somebody knows somebody who knows somebody who knows somebody who shares a community with somebody is how the economics of the world go 'round.**

My dad knew Ted from synagogue and first hired him. When I started to make money, I hired him because my dad had hired him. I didn't search online, watch content, or speak to any other financial advisor.

Ted's managed my money for nine years. To this day, I've no idea whether he has any credentials.

I don't know what credentials a financial advisor should have.

I don't know if he's been successful with others.

Ted does a great job for me. If he didn't, he wouldn't have kept our business.

But my dad didn't know he was good when he hired him. All he knew was that Ted could be trusted, which gave Ted an opportunity to prove himself—a chance other advisors, no matter how good their ads happened to be, didn't get.

By the time a sale can be measured, all the Obvious Choices have already been hired. There's no data. I don't show up as a lost lead for any other financial advisor, because I've never inquired. Ted got my business before I knew what an advisor did. Most things work this way.

All the things we conventionally think of when we think of marketing—paid ads, content, flyers, booths at events—are exciting. They're easy to teach. Easy to see. And easy to measure.

Strategically building trust, on the other hand, is nebulous. Affinity often masquerades as luck.

You can't measure the value of a single relationship formed through a board seat at a synagogue until one day you can. Until one day somebody you met (my dad) hires you. Until one day, he refers you to his son (me) and at least five other relatives.

My dad's referrals alone are worth more than $100,000 annually in fees to Ted and have generated more than $1 million for his financial advisory firm over a lifetime. And I'm sure that my dad isn't the only one.

None of this considers second order consequences either. A few minutes before I sat down to edit this section, a wealthy friend, the solo owner of a $200 million business, asked me for a referral to an investment advisor. I introduced him to Ted. That's how this stuff happens. That's how this stuff always happens.

Sitting on the board of the local synagogue doesn't sound like marketing, and yet the time he's invested there has generated remarkable financial returns.

Ted cares about his faith. His intentions aren't purely business. But still, you've gotta admit that it's a savvy move if you're a financial advisor.

Reading this back to myself, I can't help but reflect on the first two sections of this chapter with embarrassment.

The reasons my wife and I had for hiring arguably the two most important people in our family's life—our investment advisor and the guy who treated Alison for cancer—were both objectively bad. But also, very human.

———

It Hertz

My roommate moved out and took his TV with him. I had one requirement for a new TV: it needed to have pictures that moved, ideally in color.

In an attempt to learn about television technology, I typed "how to buy a TV" into Google and got 3.82 billion results in 0.62 seconds. That number doesn't make sense. So, here's a nonsense analogy: if every result was an ant, I'd have 21,000 pounds of ants.

I clicked on the first link and read the advice. Then I clicked on the next, and it gave me some of the same advice but also contradicted the first in a few places. It took about five minutes for me to reach the "ain't nobody got time for this shit" phase of my search.

Next stop: the electronics store. There were dozens of TVs. Every single one had color pictures that moved. What an amazing world we live in!

A salesman, I'll call him Todd for no reason, asked me if I wanted to buy a TV. I said yes.

"What do you like to watch?" Todd asked.

"Sports," I said.

Not sure why I said that. I don't watch much TV. These days my family doesn't even own one. Not that I don't like TV. I LOVE TV, which is kind of the point. I have a personal life philosophy to keep the special things special.

Whenever I'm at a friend's house and the TV is on, I'm amazed at the experience. "Look at how big it is! And the colors! Wait, so you get *how* many channels?" They laugh at me. I deserve it.

Television's captivating technology. There's a lot of everyday magic in our world that stops being special if we make the mistake of making it normal.

Anyway, back then I said sports. Todd told me to optimize for a hertz refresh rate. He said it makes moving images appear sharper.

Hertz refresh rate sounds made up. To this day I don't know if it's a real thing. I never looked it up. Okay, I finally looked it up just now. It does exist. According to the internet, "a higher refresh rate provides smoother motion for everything from movies and shows to live sports and gaming." Supposedly, 60 Hz is good and 120 Hz is great, whatever that means.

I walked in wanting a TV; Todd sold me one. In a matter of minutes and with a single question, he built trust via specificity, making one of the TVs in the store the Obvious Choice.

Todd's job was to sell me a TV *that day*—to provide me with the permission I needed to buy a moving pictures box. He asked a single question that allowed him to make a recommendation specific to me.

If Todd was flawed at his job, I would have hemmed and hawed. (Oh, look, a Dr. Seuss rhyme.) An unconfident salesman would have tried to impress me with his knowledge about television technology.

The "lazy mind" model, identified by the Nobel Prize–winning psychologists Daniel Kahneman and Amos Tversky, suggests that "thinking is to humans as swimming is to cats—we only do it if we have to."

Confused people don't buy. Overwhelming customers with features and specs in a vain attempt to convince them your thing is better doesn't solve their problem—it gives them more things to think about. Which causes delays.

The only part about what you do that matters is what matters to other people who aren't you.

Once you know what they want, highlight it and tell them why you're suited to solve their problem. The easier you make their decision, the more obvious the choice their purchase will be.

It starts with curiosity. Counterintuitively, the more questions you ask a customer, the more confident you appear.

Most everybody needs a good enough solution. And most solutions are good enough. However, humans don't want to admit they didn't do their research. A good rule of thumb is that if they feel they can justify to their spouse why they bought the thing based off of one fact, figure, spec, credential, or aspect of your background, they'll buy. Just one.

I wanted a TV. It needed pictures that moved, ideally in color.

But if Todd didn't ask me about sports, which allowed him to make a specific recommendation, I probably would've had to "think about it" and left because the store had like fifty TVs, and they all had pictures in color that moved. Todd's question built trust through specificity, giving me permission to buy.

I don't remember ever watching sports on the TV.

Soon after, however, I did invite a beautiful young woman with legs that screamed "I squat" named Alison back to my apartment to watch a terrible movie we'd both already seen. The pictures on the screen moved, I think. I wasn't paying attention. Neither was she.

I guess what I'm saying is that if I didn't have a TV with moving pictures I would've never invited Alison over with a cheesy line. Now she's my wife. And we have a wonderful family. Thank you for the hertz, Todd.

—

Your World ≠ Their World

A lot of people sell a product or service just as good as yours.

Most customers would be happy with the other thing just as much as your thing.

To your customers, before they become your customers, you are not as special as you think you are. Neither am I. Neither is PhD Petey McPeterson, who everybody admires because he knows so much, and isn't it annoying that his name alliterates?

When humans have problems, they look for "good enough" solutions.

Buying a thing because we think it's the best is a lie we tell ourselves.

Intuitively, we all know that we don't know what the best is for most of what we buy. And so, people don't actually want the best. Instead, they need to trust that whatever they're buying isn't bad. And people don't want cheap, they want easy. They won't admit any of this, of course. The American political scientist Herbert Simon, who first identified this phenomenon, calls this behavior "satisficing."

If all else is equal, the cheaper object usually wins. All else is never equal, though. At least it shouldn't be. That's why, if you think you're competing, you've already lost.

Most people maximize in one to three areas of expertise and satisfice in everything else—including your product or service. This concept—the juxtaposition between satisficing and maximizing—cuts at the core of our frustrations when we complain about how customers "just don't get it." It's true; they don't. And we shouldn't expect them to.

You know what designations, qualifications, and specs are important; others don't. Get educated so you can develop a good product or service, but don't expect your education or credentials to help you sell it.

There are two wrinkles in this conversation.

The first is that we don't want to admit in public that we satisfice. How we want others to believe we act is very different from how we actually act. This is why you're reading this thinking that what I'm saying doesn't apply to you. It does. It's also why doing surveys on public forums is useless.

The second is that we're actually a combination of maximizer and satisficer. In a few select areas, we do maximize. You're likely a maximizer in your area of expertise. You know what matters and what doesn't. You know the rational "good" buying reasons. Not only that, you're surrounded by people who think like you. All of this, of course, blinds you to reality.

Basically, you're too close to your own world.

—

The Dude

A man waved to me out the window of my home office. Brown hair, big smile, medium build. The Dude pointed to a van with the words, "Bolton Foods, Organic Meats & Seafood to Your Door."

"I'm doing a delivery to one of your neighbors. Whenever we do this, we ask around and see if anybody else needs anything. Do you eat meat or fish and, if so, what kinds do you like?" he said.

Ten minutes later, I packed $550 of newly bought steak and sushi-grade fish into our freezer.

In addition to affinity and specificity, familiarity is another powerful way to gain trust. It's called the mere-exposure theory[1]—the more we see something, the more we like it.

Big brands spend millions of dollars over many years to develop familiarity on a large scale. The Obvious Choice accelerates familiarity by concentrating on a very small target audience or market to create an "everywhere illusion"—strategically omnipresent to a chosen few.

I have no idea whether the Dude was *actually* making a delivery to a neighbor.

Bolton Foods could've taken a more conventional path and assumed that the only solutions were to spend money on ads, flyers, content, and booths at street festivals. If they did any of those, it would have been costly and unpredictable.

Consider their problem:

They sell high-quality meat. A lot of meat is marketed as high-quality.

In the grocery store, price matters. In retail, customers compare.

The straightest path to success isn't online marketing either. How would they stand out? Nobody would ever know that they're better because their competitors (who sell an inferior product) use the same nice-sounding words in their marketing and have bigger budgets. Sound familiar?

I imagine this is frustrating for Bolton Foods. They sell good food, on a small scale, at a justifiably premium price, to mostly uneducated consumers, in a commoditized industry where a low-quality, mass-produced, and hormone-infused product is the norm.

Great marketing often doesn't feel like marketing. It feels natural. And it happens when you work backward from the problem instead of forward from assumed solutions.

Bolton Foods became the Obvious Choice by parking a van on a street. Think about it:

1. They sell expensive meat, so

2. they need wealthy customers, and

3. most people can't accurately assess quality, but

4. rich people prioritize quality and convenience over price.

At the same time, they want to:

5. Maximize profit, and

6. avoid comparison.

Tight-knit communities follow discernible patterns. While social media can feel random and erratic, local communities are reliable and consistent.

By doing the least scalable thing, by physically showing up, the Dude cut through the noise.

It was genuine and it was human. I trusted him more than you should trust a guy who shows up with a van at your house selling meat.

When I took out my credit card to pay, he said: "I'm happy to take a credit card, but if it's no difference to you, would you mind paying with debit? That saves me 3 percent."

I paid with debit; he made an additional $16.50 in profit. Stretch that out a year and, at ten sales a day, he makes $41,000 more in profit simply by taking debit—something not possible when selling online.

Not only that, but selling online has additional hidden costs for paid ads, content, influencer outreach, and sponsorships. And selling through grocery stores is a volume game. Stores have a profit margin of 1–3 percent and obsess over price, which forces their vendors into razor-thin margins.

Physically driving to a neighborhood, parking a van, and talking to people maximizes profit by eliminating countless hidden expenses. Admittedly, it's not efficient or scalable. But there's also no middle man, no marketing cost, a more condensed delivery radius, and no transaction cost. In my most conservative estimate, this would add 10 percent profit ($55 on my sale and $137,500 a year *more* based on just ten sales a day).

The most profitable businesses are the Obvious Choice businesses.

With extra profit, you have options. You can decide to scale later. Or not.

According to Mike Michalowicz in *The Pumpkin Plan*: "Most pumpkin farmers grow ordinary pumpkins, but a small portion grows colossal. They only change a few things and the pumpkin responds with colossal growth. Entrepreneurs change a few things, and their business responds with colossal growth."

Here are a few things that the top pumpkin farmers focus on:

- Match the seed to the dirt. More isn't better.
- Focus on strong sprouts. Ignore weak ones.
- Water the same spot. Frequently.
- Weed constantly.

Great analogy.

—

Just because you can sell online, it doesn't mean you have to. And what you don't hear about enough is how much more difficult and expensive it is to sell online when you're new.

It's not a one-or-the-other thing though. Online and local marketing like this can be combined to maximize leverage. Building trust through familiarity is a powerful way to reduce the cost of customer acquisition.

If I were Bolton Foods, here's how I'd scale:

I'd park branded vans in different sections of well-selected neighborhoods for several weeks in a row. When there, my team would talk to whomever is around and drop flyers in mailboxes (if legal in the area).

Delivery vans on the street are an indicator that somebody's getting a delivery—that a neighbor trusts the service (even if we don't know our neighbor and even if nobody is *actually* getting a delivery).

Once the vans became a familiar sight on the street, we'd send physical mailings in addition to online advertisements through both geotargeted search and social media to the same group of people. Response rate would increase. Customer acquisition costs would decrease.

If we did this, Bolton Foods might not be known to the internet at large, but to the neighborhoods that we target, we'd be everywhere. It'd appear that *everybody was buying*—that we're bigger than we are.

Market deep, not wide. You're better off sending one letter to a hundred well-selected mailboxes every week for five weeks than you are sending five hundred letters to five hundred mailboxes one time.

After three to four weeks, Bolton Foods would have customers.

Whenever we make a delivery, we'd leave notes wherever legal in the area that say: "We just delivered local, fresh, hormone-free steak and fish to your neighbor. We save money when we make deliveries close by and like to pass along the savings with a discount special to you. So, here's a discount code to use before the end of the week for next week's delivery."

A few more examples . . .

If you're a real estate agent and have a listing, host an open house the night before for "nosy neighbors." Tell people to attend at a specific time because you'll be sharing the listing price and why it was chosen and what it means for the value of other houses on the street.

Send invites to nearby houses. Buy some wine and cheese and overpriced water in glass bottles. Hand everybody who attends a letter talking about how familiar you are with the neighborhood. Try to get their addresses and emails in exchange for the promise of a price breakdown of future houses for sale in the neighborhood.

Follow up with a customized message: "Hey, we met at the nosy neighbor event. No rush, but whenever you're ready to consider selling your home, please give me a call." Touch base every time a new house goes on the market (even if it isn't your listing) with the price and what it means for other houses nearby.

If you're a personal trainer, take the bus to a rich neighborhood and knock on doors. Say that you were in between clients and in the neighborhood (none of this is a lie) and figured you'd see if you could answer any questions on health or fitness.

While doing this, post flyers with the same message on public billboards and in local cafes. Leave a letter in each mailbox if legal in the area. Go back to the same streets for two to three weeks. Then begin mailing flyers and sending paid online ads targeted to that community.

If you own a landscaping business, get your crews to park your work trucks on key streets in the weeks before grass-cutting season begins. Knock on doors and say that you're in the area giving quotes for neighbors and ask if they'd like a no-commitment assessment and quote right now.

Once you get one house to hire you, put signs up in public areas and on public notice boards that say: "We're already cutting lawns in your neighborhood and can give you a cheaper rate because we have to travel less. Give us a call for a free quote and ask for the (*insert neighborhood name*) discount." Begin mailing letters and sending online ads targeted to the same people with the same message.

The Dude came back two weeks later and parked on my street. I waved.

My neighbor David was outside. He asked how the steak was. I told him it was great. David bought meat from the Dude and paid with debit.

There was a knock on our door two weeks before Christmas. It was the Dude.

"Hey! Just checking in to see if you're all stocked for the holidays and any meals you might be hosting," he said.

Market deep, not wide. Work once, sell twice.

The Dude abides.

Finding Perfect Customers with the Marble Method

The logical question that follows from the Bolton Foods example is how to know, metaphorically or physically, what street to park your van on? Where do you find your perfect customers?

I don't have an answer, but I do have a process. It's called the Marble Method.

The easiest way to find a lost marble in the grass is by dropping another one. Because marbles are round, they naturally roll to the bottom of a slope. When you drop a second marble, it follows contours in the ground invisible to our eyes, the same way as the first.

The Marble Method works backward from what you have to find more of the same.

First, split a piece of paper into two columns:

1. Most Valuable Customers
2. Most Liked Customers

Under "Most Valuable," write the names of your top ten customers based on lifetime value.

Under "Most Liked," write the names of the ten customers that you liked the most.

Rewrite the names that appear on both sides of the page below. My guess is that there will be three or four.

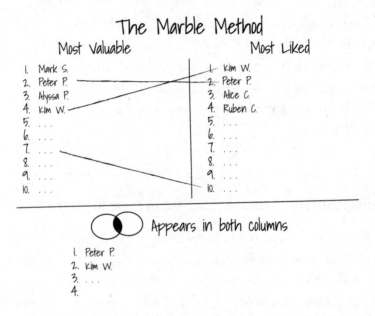

Aim to re-create more of your best customers by working backward. Begin by writing down your top ten most valuable. Then your most liked. There are likely to be three or four that cross over. Deconstruct who they are for clues on where to find more customers like them.

Then deconstruct who they are, where they live, what they like, and how they found you. In many cases, you can simply ask them. A few questions to consider:

- Where do they live?
- What communities, foundations, or societies are they active in?

- Whom do they admire/follow?
- What books, magazines, podcasts, or any other type of media do they consume?
- What other stuff do they buy?
- If local, what other stores do they frequent? What vendors do they use?
- What are their hobbies?

Collate the responses and look for patterns. That's where you park your van.

You can download a Marble Method worksheet to find your perfect customers at www.JonathanGoodman.com/Marble.

—

Beating Michael Jordan

Want to know how to beat Michael Jordan?

You sure as hell don't play basketball.

In his prime, Michael Jordan was the best. Challenge him at his own game, you'll lose. Bolton Foods' equivalent to Michael Jordan is Costco.

In my neighborhood, Bolton Foods is beating Costco by playing a game Costco can't play—by playing their own game—by being the big fish in a small pond—by being the Dude.

Despite what you see online, trust through community, specificity, and familiarity drive more sales, easier sales, and more profitable sales than any piece of content, script, or advertisement on their own.

The tricky part about trust is that it won't feel like anything is happening until, one day, it happens all at once.

There's a few lessons we can pull out here:

The first is to get out of your own head. Most of what matters to you is irrelevant to the people you sell to.

The second is that because trust is harder to see than most people imagine, it's more lucrative than most assume.

The third is that starting and scaling are two different games. When you start, optimize for profit. There are a lot of problems that can be solved with money, and a lot more that arise when you don't have enough.

There are a lot of ways to market and sell with technology. You cannot, however, do them all. The easiest approach could be as simple as parking a van on a street.

Next, how to cheat (well) at blackjack.

CHAPTER 3

Success Shouldn't Be a Surprise

Terrible Story, Great Life — Neon Monsters — Cheating (Well) at Blackjack — Connecting the Dots Backward

Against-all-odds success stories get shared as gospel. "If they can do it, so can you." These inspirational examples are wonderful and can be quite useful.

What's also useful is the awareness that being surprised when something works is a bad thing.

Curated selections of successful stories skew our reality.

—

A speaker onstage tells the inspirational story of a podcaster who, against all odds, made it big. Supposedly this guy, a sales coach, had fifty listeners in year one and could barely afford his tiny apartment.

By year five, he had five hundred listeners. And at year seven, the show caught fire and he had one million downloads. What grit! What a testament to believing in oneself, doing the work, and pushing through against all odds.

But also, this dude worked for free for six years.

And, yeah, it worked out. That's why we're talking about him. But it also might not have. For most, it doesn't. I'd like to talk about that instead.

His story was shared because it's remarkable. It was remarked upon because it was an outlier event.

The more unexpected the success, the bigger the outlier, and the better the story. While we might learn bits and pieces from outliers, it's a mistake to expect similar results from doing the same things. **Success stories are visible; failures are invisible. The resulting effects are a combination of overoptimistic thinking and correlation/causation errors.**

Survivorship bias assumes that success tells the whole story and ignores past failures. Nobody speaks onstage about people who take insane risks, fail miserably, and live their lives as abject failures in beds of their own making.

The only reason we're hearing about our hero is that his success was unexpected.

The odds were stacked against him.

Bad decisions, however, can still result in positive outcomes. A 95 percent chance of failure still has a 5 percent chance of success, after all.

In math, 20 x 1 is the same as 1 x 20, but in real life, it rarely is. For example, you can raise the average level of wealth of everyone in a baseball stadium by $100,000 simply by having Jeff Bezos walk in. As Rory Sutherland wrote in *Alchemy*, "A single rogue outlier can lead to an extraordinary distortion of reality." We must be careful when consuming sensational stories.

The first step to seeing through the outlier illusion is to understand what makes for a good story. After I outline all the elements to look out for with outliers, I'll share a process for you to guarantee your own good luck.

—

Terrible Story, Great Life

It's impressive hearing about somebody winning with the odds stacked against them, but a big part of me always wonders, "Why did the odds have to be stacked against you in the first place?"

Struggle and sacrifice and hopelessness aren't necessary for success. They're necessary for story. There's a difference.

Books featuring people who have done well (not this one, but most books) don't celebrate outliers because they're useful examples; they do it because they sell books. Life isn't a story, but stories are how we talk about life.

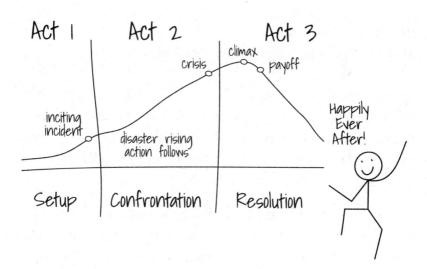

As we've learned from Joseph Campbell's The Hero's Journey, *at its core, every story follows the same three-part structure. Act one is the setup where the main character embarks on a journey. Act two is confrontation, where the struggle escalates. Act three is the resolution, where everybody lives happily ever after.*

Outliers who overcome create compelling narratives. On the other hand, a lot of people win without adversity. We just don't hear about them.

For a story to be impactful, it needs three acts. I'll use our hero from the start of this chapter, the podcaster, to illustrate each one.

Act One: Setup
The main characters are introduced and an "inciting incident" propels them on a journey.

Our hero starts a podcast from his one-bedroom apartment.

Act Two: Confrontation
An unexpected plot twist leads to a disaster and crisis, escalating until it all feels hopeless.

Our hero struggles to pay his bills. Nobody's listening to his podcast.

Act Three: Resolution
The payoff, where everybody lives happily ever after.

After six years, he gets his break and goes viral, getting one million downloads. The story ends. Our brains make up the rest as we assume he's now living on a private island somewhere wearing fuzzy slippers, surrounded by supermodels, and eating an endless supply of overpriced caviar.

Humans are thought to have first appeared about 300,000 years ago. The first cave paintings date back 40,000 years. Ancient writing systems seem to date back 4,600 years, and the printing press is only 560 years old.

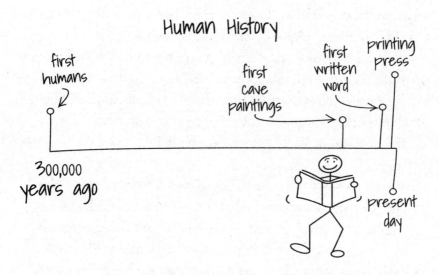

For 99.99 percent of human history, the brain evolved to operate without the help of the written word. Our brains didn't develop to pass notes to one another. They evolved to tell stories around fires.

Simplified, almost every story follows this three-act structure. In real life, however, act two is unnecessary; conflict, disaster, and hopelessness aren't requirements for success, and act three doesn't exist—there's no happily ever after.

Andy Warhol once said that "you can be watching TV and see Coca-Cola, and know that the President drinks Coke, Liz Taylor drinks Coke, and just think, you can drink Coke, too. A Coke is a Coke and no amount of money can get you a better Coke." What's true of Coca-Cola is also true of the morbid reality of life: That there's one day and the next day. Once those are done, more days come; until they don't.

It's true that some people have more and others have less. Just remember that the more or the less isn't what gives our experience on this rock its flavor. Life's a road, not a destination. Get in the car and go for a drive. What kind of car? It doesn't matter; they all drive the speed limit. Explore. Have fun. Just make sure there's always something nice to look at out the window.

It's perfectly okay that there won't be a book written about your life. Better, even. Nobody writes books about lives well-lived because they follow routine fundamentals that result in boringly good outcomes. Basically, they make for bad stories.

Think about it. Would you read a book if this was the premise?

So-and-so woke up, went to pee, drank a coffee, fed the kids, and took them to school. He then exercised, drank another coffee, and didn't get lost trying to do everything perfectly, executing on a few reliably good-enough and well-selected daily tasks. Once done, he ate his veggies, went for a walk after dinner with his family, chatted with a neighbor, read some fiction, said "I love you" to his wife (he never forgot to say "I love you" to his wife), and went to bed. He didn't get distracted and followed this routine more or less on repeat for a few decades. Over time, his efforts were consistently good enough, and they added up. There were tough times, of course, but overall he was happy, healthy, loved, and fulfilled. It worked for him, and it'll work for you, too!

Not exactly *New York Times* best-seller material. Great life, though.

———

Neon Monsters

From 1995 to 2018, Monster Beverage—purveyors of only the finest sugar-filled, neon-colored caffeine bombs—was one of the best-performing NASDAQ stocks. In that time, the stock increased an astounding 300,000 percent. If you invested $10,000 in 1995 into Monster, you'd have more than $30 million in 2018.

Imagine what life must've been like owning that stock during its meteoric rise? Every day opening the newspaper, smiling at the bucket of money you (yet again) made, telling your boss to suck it when you quit your unfulfilling job, making love to your wife in the middle of the day. Ah, if you could only go back in time.

But also, during Monster's meteoric rise, its stock traded *below* its previous high 95 percent of the time. Four separate times it lost 50 percent of its value.

I'm not a finance guy. When people ask me why I became a personal trainer, I jokingly tell them that the guidance counselor in high school asked me to count to twelve. I lost count at seven and told her "three more." She handed me a clipboard and a pair of sweatpants and said, "Have at it."

If you're also not a finance guy, here's what the above means: the best-performing stock of the past two decades appeared to be failing 95 percent of the time. According to finance journalist Morgan Housel, "What now looks like a slam-dunk story was, at any given time in the last twenty years, an easy story to criticize."

No telling your boss to suck it. No quitting your unfulfilling job. No daytime lovemaking (well, maybe some, but any afternoon delights would've been unrelated). None of that. Owning the stock would've been filled with doubt and worry. There's no free lunch—even if you got lucky or somehow knew in 1995 that humans were going to really, really love ingesting sugar-filled, neon-colored caffeine bombs.

The *New Yorker* essayist Tim Kreider wrote: "Life is an adventure, not a test. There are no correct answers in the back of the book; we don't get to find out what was behind door number two; we never even know whether we won. If you want some guarantee that everything will turn out all right and you'll have no regrets, it's not an adventure you want; it's a theme park."

Good decisions don't always work out. Our world is too complex and therefore too unpredictable.

Success is 50 percent luck and 50 percent timing. The other half is smarts and skill.

The obvious question that follows is how to get some of this luck for ourselves.

To find the answer, let's now turn our attention to the American mathematics professor who pioneered many modern applications of probability theory, including the harnessing of very small correlations for reliable financial gain. Said simply: he beat the casino.

——

Cheating (Well) at Blackjack

Edward Thorp ran two of the most successful hedge funds of all time, built the first wearable computer to beat roulette, and developed the original method of counting cards to win at blackjack.

None of those things are as interesting to me as his betting strategy, when he knew that he had a statistical edge. Thorp was overconservative. He described his approach in his autobiography, *A Man for All Markets*:

> There were two main approaches we could adopt when we sat down to play in the casinos. One, which I call wild, involved betting the table limit whenever the advantage to the player exceeded some small figure, say 1 percent. This typically wins the most money, but fluctuations in wealth may be violent, and a large bankroll is required to ride out big losses.

Okay, this is important. Let's make sense of it.

Imagine a competitive downhill skier. When he's aggressive, he has a 20 percent chance of winning but also a 20 percent chance of crashing and getting hurt. If he gets injured, he's eliminated from competition moving forward.

How many races out of ten do you think he'll win?

The answer isn't two. It's not even one.

Mathematically, the reckless skier will win 0.79 races out of 10. Since the number of races won must be a whole number, technically the correct answer is zero.

We celebrate recklessness when it pays off, ignoring all the times that it doesn't. Accepting an insane level of risk is a trade-off professional athletes knowingly accept that I invite you to ignore.

Thorp's financial backers urged him to bet big whenever he had the advantage. He refused. When the odds were in his favor he increased his bets conservatively but never put himself at risk of busting.

Let's say that you make a great decision with a 70 percent chance of success. That's insanely good odds. Still, three out of ten times, you'll be dealt a bad hand. Keep at it and the odds of success will eventually play out in your favor. Spiritual people refer to this turning of the tides of fortune as karma. I call it math.

Thorp's backer, Manny, got impatient with his conservative betting. Frustrated, he sat down at the table beside Thorp. They both wore costumes to avoid being recognized. I'm not making this up. Old-time Vegas was wild. Here's what happened next, in Thorp's own words:

> I cashed out and wended my way back to the tables to watch horror-stricken as Manny, feeling lucky and refusing to stop, poured back thousands of dollars. For me, blackjack was a game of math, not luck. Any luck, good or bad, would be random, unpredictable, and short-term. In the long run it would be unimportant. Manny didn't see it that way. When I tried to dislodge him he cried excitedly, "I . . . will . . . not . . . leave . . . this . . . place!" In the forty-five minutes or so that it took to pry him loose, he lost back the entire $11,000 that he had won. Even so, when we returned to our hotel that

evening with my winnings, we were ahead $13,000 [about $131,000 in 2023] so far on the trip.

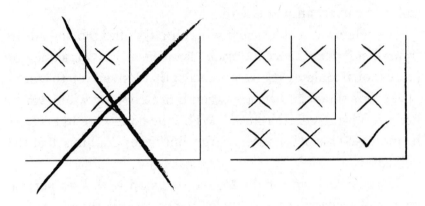

The only way to guarantee good luck is to skew the odds of success in your favor and stay in the game long enough for the odds to play out.

It's impossible to win if you get knocked out of the game. In the immediate, luck is random. In the long term, luck, as Thorp said, is "unimportant."

Greed is a short-term game played by short-term people. Going all-in, even if you think the odds are in your favor, very often leads to ruin. Aesop was right—the tortoise always beats the hare.

Connecting the Dots Backward

As the ultimate outlier, Steve Jobs said: "You can't connect the dots looking forward; you can only connect them looking backward. So, you have to trust that the dots will somehow connect in your future."

This is such an important point to internalize that I'm going to hit you with a few more quotes from people whose work has stood the test of time.

From Daniel Kahneman, a Nobel Prize–winning behavioral psychologist: "The idea that the future is unpredictable is undermined every day by the ease with which the past is explained."

From Nassim Nicholas Taleb, the author of *Black Swan: The Impact of the Highly Improbable*: "We humans fool ourselves by constructing flimsy accounts of the past and believing they are true."

From Arthur Conan Doyle in the Sherlock Holmes short story "The Problem of Thor Bridge": "It is easy to be wise after the event."

And finally, from the Danish philosopher Søren Aabye Kierkegaard: "We understand life backward but live it forward."

It's easy to predict things after they've happened because the human brain isn't equipped to comprehend our modern world's complexity. In an attempt to make sense of it all, we post-rationalize, fabricating narratives that smooth out the edges of life, assuming patterns that don't exist.

In hindsight, everything seems obvious. In reality, nothing is as simple in the moment as history makes it seem.

Nobody knows what the future will bring. The people who become the Obvious Choice measure success with a long lens. With the proper habits, they skew the odds in their favor and, with a long-enough time-horizon, the odds always work themselves out.

Monster isn't the exception; it's the rule. Netflix's stock price increased 35,000 percent from 2002 to 2018. It also traded below its previous high on 94 percent of those days. Amazon lost

90 percent of its value from 2000 to 2002. On September 3, 2020, Apple lost $180 billion in company value. And so on.

The correct lesson to take from outliers is that their success isn't a straight line; it's a goddamn roller coaster run by some carnie chugging chocolate milk in the sun.

Next, let's talk about the people and things that affect us most, and that most of us ignore.

—

CHAPTER 4

Fix What's Inside
Your Fence First

*Blinded to the Truth — Janet's Bridge Posse —
Breezy — When Faking It Doesn't Result in
Making It — Advice from a Billionaire — $200 Is
$200 Is $200*

O ur social media bubble represents maybe 0.01 percent of
what goes on in the world that affects us and likely closer to
0.0000001 percent of what goes on in the world at large.

There's ego involved, sure. But it's also important to point out
the obvious yet admittedly hard-to-remember-in-the-moment fact
that whatever you see on that addictive device in your pocket is
less important than what isn't on it.

—

Mujeres Movimiento is a charity that supports battered women in
Sayulita, Mexico. It removes them from bad situations and helps
them become independent by launching small business ventures.

My wife, Alison, and her mom decided to raise $10,000 to buy
them a much-needed van through a number of initiatives, including making and selling earrings.

Alison took nice photos of the jewelry, spoke of the cause, and posted it to her 1,600 Instagram followers and 3,400 Facebook friends. "Pay what you can. Anything helps," she wrote.

No response.

Maybe it was the pictures, she thought.

So, Alison took better pictures, rewrote the story, and posted again.

And again, no response.

Then she sent a personal message to ten friends and ex-colleagues. Eight out of ten responded and bought earrings. One of them sent her $500. And a few even said, "You know, I thought that I saw something about this on Instagram."

Through the sale of earrings and a few other initiatives, Mujeres Movimiento bought the van. They've jump-started forty-seven job-creation programs in the Banderas Bay area and counting.

Posting on the internet and praying to El Zucko, the god of social media, that somebody will pay attention, respond, and ask to buy your thing doesn't work.

Hiding behind your keyboard trying to craft the perfect message doesn't work.

Human Avoidance Marketing (HAM) *doesn't work.*

Whenever somebody asks me for advice, because they're having trouble selling early on in their journey, I respond with a question: "How many people did you speak to today?"

—

Blinded to the Truth

It's impossible to miss the huge 100,000-square-foot gym from the highway. Twenty thousand members pay a premium to work out there. Management hired me to help the struggling twenty-person trainer team.

Jenny, average height, blonde hair, black exercise pants, and a blue tank top—standard personal trainer attire—raised her hand to ask a question: "A lot of us are struggling to get clients. Is there any advice you have for growing our social media?"

The gym had twenty thousand paying members. A trainer needs twenty clients working out between one and three times a week for a full schedule. I usually avoid public math, but this one's easy:

Jenny needs to convert 0.1 percent of the existing members into personal training clients.

And yet, her question told me that she assumed the only way to generate business was to convince random people on the internet to buy.

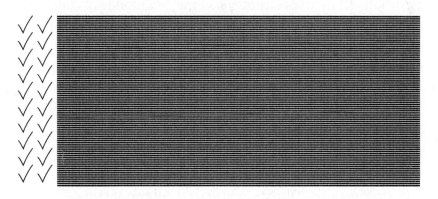

Out of 20,000 paying members, Jenny only needed twenty clients.
Most people have more than enough leads in their real life.
Look there first before trying to impress the internet.

She showed me her phone and told me about her posting strategy. Her account had five thousand followers and 1,350 posts. The page was beautifully branded with a clearly defined style and color theme featuring an array of recipes, meal-prepping tips, and exercise demonstrations.

"What can I do better on IG to get more clients?" she asked.

"Have you ever gotten a client from social media?" I responded.

"No," she replied.

I paused to let the silence in the room sink in.

It's impossible for me to know how much time Jenny had spent on her account—hundreds of hours easily, maybe thousands. And she hadn't gotten a single customer from it. Despite all this, she's firm in her conviction that there's some secret she's missing. That the problem is her content. That IG's the way to get clients. That if she just works a bit harder on her social media, she'll uncover the mystery.

Social media is, in the words of Morpheus in *The Matrix*, "the world that has been pulled over your eyes to blind you to the truth."

It seduces us into thinking that if we figure out how to get attention online from strangers, money will follow. While there might be some overlap, **endlessly publishing content to the abyss in an attempt to get famous on the internet is a gloriously inefficient way to build a business.**

In many ways, *The Matrix* isn't fiction. It's a documentary.

———

I did a tour of the gym before the meeting. Hundreds of members were working out. Only two trainers were with clients. No other staff were present. Thirty minutes later, all twenty trainers materialized in the room. Where were they?

As it turns out, many of them were sitting in their breakroom with the door closed, scrolling social media and creating content while they waited for our meeting about lead generation and sales. Meanwhile, *literally outside their door*, hundreds of potential customers were being ignored.

Most people claim they want to be an influencer, but the truth is that they'd be happier with a simple life, impacting the lives of their customers, making a good living, and enjoying their spare time with family and friends.

But everybody's different.

Some want to work hard and make as big an impact as possible, and others are happy to do their thing in their quiet corner of the world. Neither person's right, and neither person's wrong.

What's universally true is that nobody you don't know will be impressed if you ignore social media and focus on real-life humans for a while. In our backward world, what's bad for our ego is often great for our wallet.

Admittedly, Jenny's example is extreme. Most businesses don't already have twenty thousand paying customers to pull from. The advice, however, is the same: before trying to impress people you've never met (and wouldn't care about if you did), open the door.

I asked Jenny one final question: "What do you think is more valuable to your business—five thousand random people worldwide who have kind of heard of you, or twenty wealthy and well-connected people who are already in this building right now?"

The air left the room. For those struggling trainers, the answer became obvious.

I think that they secretly knew what they should have been doing all along.

—

Janet's Bridge Posse

My mom was invited to Janet's fitness class by a friend. She told me that the group was—this was hilarious—a "posse."

Janet's in her forties and started playing bridge at the local club. In the most unsurprising turn of events ever, she was the youngest there. And because she's noticeably fit, the table talk turned to fitness.

The contrast between Jenny in the previous story and Janet's approach provides a useful Obvious Choice case study.

Janet's entire fitness business was built from that bridge club. It's run with a WhatsApp text message group whose members include fifty-plus local women aged fifty to seventy-five.

She doesn't use email, let alone have a social media account. The WhatsApp group organizes exercise classes, and its members use the same group to schedule get-togethers like bridge games. Janet doesn't do any marketing—her clients invite others to join the, oh geez, fine, I'll say it, "posse."

Just because you can get a customer on the internet doesn't mean you have to.

To your bottom line, it doesn't matter whether they live a block away or they spend their weekends sipping yerba maté in Pocitos, a beachside barrio of Montevideo in Uruguay. The only difference is that **the more distant the connection, the harder it is to get customers, retain them, and get referrals from them.**

Kinship is a relationship that forms when people feel connected because they live close, have a common interest, share a religious

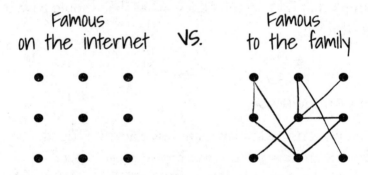

When your community members are close to one another (either physically or metaphorically), the shared kinship results in improved connections, which results in more referrals and retention through community. On the other hand, working with a disconnected customer base, usually online, forces you to create every customer independent of one another. In addition, there are fewer built-in forces keeping them around.

affiliation, or any of a thousand other uncommon commonalities that align us with one another.

A recommendation from a stranger gets ignored. That same recommendation from a stranger who happens to be in the same trusted group as you is something to check out.

Janet has a fabulously humble business. She's making a difference. She's not rich but she has enough. And I don't know this for sure, but I bet that she gets freshly baked lemon squares made with love *all the time.*

Doing great work in your local community and earning a modest-yet-good-enough living so that you can go home at the end of the day to a loving spouse, gifts of freshly baked treats, and a good book sounds weird in our modern hustle culture where you're told that if you're not getting ahead, you're not doing enough. But, for many of us, this lifestyle appeals.

———

Breezy

Daniel Breez is an accountant with a microscopically small market.

He specializes in working with coaches who live in Ontario, Canada, charge US dollars, and sell high-ticket packages to international clients.

Daniel's path began conventionally as a staff accountant before accepting a role as the finance manager of a skin care company. In addition to his full-time job, he took on a few private clients. One of them was a coach.

He showed this person how to write off expenses, charge/remit appropriate sales taxes, and convert US dollars to Canadian with a more favorable rate than the rip-off exchange his bank offered.

Daniel saved his client thousands of dollars. His client was thrilled and introduced Daniel to his business coach who invited Daniel to give a presentation to the group.

There's a saying that goes, "the riches are in the niches." When you're focused on serving a specific group of people with specific needs, you can quickly become the Obvious Choice by tailoring your marketing and product to their unique needs in ways larger competitors can't.

A few more examples:

If you're a student tutor, specialize in helping kids from one school district qualify for a few key college programs. You'll know which schools to network in, understand the exact requirements to prepare the kids for, and build connections within the college enrollment departments.

If you're in lawn maintenance, target a few key neighborhoods. Become known by organizing things like volunteer park cleanups and by parking your branded vehicles on the street whenever they aren't in use. By knowing the neighborhood well, you'll be able to deliver quotes quickly. In addition, your profits will be higher if your crews have multiple houses to service close to one another.

If you're in fitness, only work with postnatal military wives who have had at least one C-section and currently live on base. You'll know where to find them, what words appeal, what pain points to create content around, and how to build your programming and support systems. By working with one type of client, you'll also be able to productize and operationalize your services faster for scale.

Within six months, Daniel had a big enough book of clients to leave his full-time finance manager job and start a micro-practice.

___

When Faking It Doesn't Result in Making It

The best way to ensure you're for no one is to say you're for everyone. Counterintuitively, the more people you exclude, the better.

I just googled "personal trainer accountant." The first result was a website from an Australian firm owned by a woman named Linda.

Her official tagline is "Strategies & Solutions for Business." That doesn't tell me much. I clicked around her website and found a tab that lists the industries she serves. I'm about to list everything that was there. Please don't read the rest of this paragraph. Skip to the next section. After this big block of text there's a space. After that space, the book continues. Skip everything until that next space. Again, do not read this. Please, stop reading. This is painful. Okay, I warned you. According to the website, here are all the things that Linda "specializes" in: builders and related trades including plumbers, electricians, and carpenters, musicians and artists, hairdressers and barbers, restaurants and bars, cafes and coffee shops, beauty therapists and nail technicians, lawn mowing contractors, landscape gardeners, tradespeople, franchisees and franchisors, retailers, medical, gyms and personal trainers, dog wash and pet grooming, real estate agents, pet shops, florists, motels, automotive mechanics, travel agents, cleaners, importers, masseurs and wellness centers, computer consultants and IT, mortgage brokers, manufacturers, hotels and bars. Are you still here? I hope you didn't read all that. But if you did, I'm sorry and want to make it up to you with a joke: There's this super secretive Indian restaurant. It's so secretive that you have to sign a legal agreement before eating there. They call it a *naan* disclosure agreement. Hahaha. Okay, moving on.

Perhaps most interesting about all this is that Linda probably provides a great accounting service for gym owners and personal trainers. But because of how she markets, she's not the Obvious Choice and has to work harder and spend more money to get clients.

Daniel, on the other hand, runs a small, thriving, highly profitable accounting business optimized for his lifestyle. He doesn't do any marketing. The dude doesn't even have a website. New clients fill out a Google form.

The tighter you target, the clearer your vision, the simpler the execution, and the bigger your profit margin.

That's because we as consumers place more value on a service that does one thing than we do on that same service that does the same one thing plus any other thing.

Up until this point, it might sound like I'm making an argument to settle. To accept mediocrity. To not go for it. But what if you have big hopes and dreams?

—

Advice from a Billionaire

I'm not a billionaire. My businesses aren't going to change the world. Peter Thiel, on the other hand, is part of the three-comma club. Paradoxically, his advice for entrepreneurs who want to make a big impact is to both think and start small.

Thiel, the cofounder of PayPal and the first investor into Facebook (now Meta), in a talk he gave at Stanford University, said, "When you're starting a company, you're starting small, so you want to get a large share of your market quickly." In his book *Zero to One*, he wrote, "The most successful companies make the core progression—to first dominate a specific niche and then scale to adjacent markets."

PayPal started with thirty thousand power sellers on eBay.

Facebook started with ten thousand students at Harvard.

Phil Knight started Nike by selling running shoes out of the trunk of his Plymouth Valiant at weekend track meets.

———

Daniel Breez, who we met earlier, started as the accountant for high-ticket, online fitness coaches in Ontario. It took him six months to gain a dominant market share. Then he expanded his micro-practice to serve all high-ticket coaches in the province. What comes next for him? We'll have to wait and see. But he's in an ideal spot.

Dominating small markets leads to larger triumphs.

The best way to execute an idea so big that it could one day change the world is to start by becoming the Obvious Choice for a small group of people. By fixing what's inside your fence first.

One final example . . .

What about business models with constraints that make them difficult to run as small enterprises from the start?

———

$200 Is $200 Is $200

Love Your Centre (www.loveyourcentre.ca) is a specialty cleaning, refinishing, and restoration company.

It's a big operation that requires a lot of space, handling of chemicals, pick-up/drop-off infrastructure, and a large advertising budget. Deep-cleaning is an impossible business to run small. The economics don't work.

None of this changes the fact that being a clear winner in a small market is the easiest business to grow and most profitable to run. Love Your Centre found the cheat code by launching twelve distinct brands.

Love Your Rug

Love Your Leather

Love Your Carpet

Love Your Shoes

Love Your Tailor

Love Your Dress

Love Your Purse

Love Your Coat

Love Your Luggage

Love Your Duct

Love Your Gear (hockey
equipment)

Love Your Drapery

Each brand has its own version of a templated website, search engine optimization, phone number, and paid advertising.

Used hockey equipment smells like sewage mixed with rat poison that's gone moldy after being left out in the rain. Despite demand for cleaning, seasonality, combined with the cost of running a hockey equipment cleaning service, are difficult problems to overcome.

Having a process for cleaning the gear in an already existing deep-cleaning warehouse makes sense for logistics and operational efficiency. For marketing, not so much.

One more thing I stumbled upon during my research. Check this out.

They even have an Air Jordan Restoration service within the Love Your Shoes subniche. So smart.

All money counts the same—$200 is $200 is $200. Whether a customer comes as a result of a satellite brand or the main brand is irrelevant. The tweak of promoting Love Your Gear (and others) as separate brands was a simple magic trick performed by Love Your Centre that made it the Obvious Choice for countless adjacent markets.

Once hired, the same truck picks up a wide range of items: a rug from one house, a purse from another, and hockey gear from the last, transporting them to the same cleaning depot.

—

Fixing what's inside your fence means you build from your strengths, not limit your vision.

You need to be able to do something that others either can't or are unwilling to do. Thiel's advice is to find a market not already heavily contested by strong competitors. One you can win with few resources simply because you're willing to focus on it and others aren't.

In many cases, this means a niche in a broader category that the leaders aren't serving well. Then, over time, as you acquire more resources, you can strategically expand to adjacent markets if you want.

First, think about what you do in a general sense. Then think about a unique customer you had and how you adapted your product or service slightly for them. Can you expand on that? Can you turn that unique variant into a focus?

—

It's okay to want to change the world.

And it's okay to not want to change the world.

Either way, if you want to become the Obvious Choice, it starts with fixing what's inside your fence first.

Next, the one thing you can do that computers can't, and won't ever, be able to do.

CHAPTER 5

Tech Changes, Humans Don't

Virtual Humans — Printer's Devil — The Parade
Problem — The Power of Not Making Sense

The problem with technological innovation isn't that it doesn't work; it's that it works the same for everybody.

What appears to improve scalability, increase production quality, and reach results is increased competition and commoditization. If you can do it, so can everybody else. The problem gets worse with every new tool we *have* to use or miss out.

Computers thrive when they're efficient. Humans thrive when we're strategically (in)efficient.

Dabbling is the secret to success. Aimless exploration is the pathway to discovery.

The harder it is to figure out where our unique perspective came from, the better. You're going for the hair-sticking-up, goose-bumps, holy-shit-where-did-that-come-from sorta stuff.

—

In 2022, I wanted to hire an urban vegetable gardening consultant.

To find help for the garden, I asked our community Facebook group if anybody had a referral. Nobody did. One person recommended TheSpruce.com. The banner atop their site promoted two thousand how-to projects.

By this point, all I knew about gardening was that dirt was involved.

It's estimated that the internet stores 44 trillion gigabytes of data. If you wanted to download all that, it would take you 40 billion years. A number that big is impossible to comprehend. For context, the earth is about 4.5 billion years old.

Information overwhelm is an impossible problem to overcome. And it's getting worse, exponentially. The paradoxical result of infinite content is that it becomes harder to use.

"In a world deluged by irrelevant information," said the historian Yuval Noah Harari in the line that begins his book *21 Lessons for the 21st Century*, "Clarity is power." Harari goes on to say, "Censorship works not by blocking the flow of information, but rather by flooding people with disinformation and distractions." When we're overwhelmed, we retreat to the safety of what we already believe to be true.

Not knowing what kind of veggies I wanted to grow, how to assess my soil quality, or even that soil quality was a thing, my summed-up thoughts clicking through The Spruce website were, once again, "Ain't nobody got time for this shit."

Since nobody I trusted could refer me to a consultant, I closed my browser and googled "Toronto Urban Vegetable Gardening Coach." A few websites appeared. I didn't read them. How could I have judged them anyway? So, I filled out their forms and sent inquiries. Then I found an Instagram account, ignored the posts, and sent a message.

Everybody responded, came to my house, and sent a proposal. I didn't know how to compare them and picked the guy I liked the most. Luay Ghafari showed up two days later to analyze my soil, sunlight, and discuss a planting schedule.

—

"The best minds of my generation are thinking about how to make people click ads," said Jeff Hammerbacher in the book *Chaos Monkeys*. Hammerbacher led the data team at Facebook. Technology changes, he points out, are too fast.

Content's impossibly overwhelming. Algorithms are mysterious. The forces working against you are absurd. You're guaranteed to be behind if you try to stay up to date. Also, it's straight-up exhausting. Keeping up with whatever Silicon Valley profiteers decide to come out with this week is not how I want to live my life.

There's a lot going on right now. I don't know when "right now" is for you because I wrote this in the past. We're not even in the same year together. And still, I know that there's a lot going on for you. There always is. But the important things don't change. Let's talk about those.

First, we need to discuss trust online. From there, we'll talk about standing out in a sea of sameness. And we'll wrap it up with the single thing you must do to thrive in a world driven by algorithms, no matter how advanced they become. Let's dig in.

—

Virtual Humans

When Jon Stewart challenged Jim Cramer, the host of CNBC's *Mad Money*, about the mistakes, contradictory information, and insane predictions he constantly makes, Cramer said, "Look, we've got seventeen hours of live TV a day to do."[1]

To which Stewart replied, "Maybe you could cut down on that?" But Cramer can't, obviously.

The internet needs constant feeding. I don't trust it anymore. The data shows that I'm not alone.

According to the 2021 Nielsen Trust in Advertising Study, 88 percent of people trust recommendations from people they know (word of mouth). Conversely, only 23 percent of people trust ads from influencers.

———

Trust in online media is shrinking at a blistering pace. This will continue.

Social media self-selects for divisiveness and extremism. Rapid news cycles are working 24/7 and result in unsubstantiated claims that become wrongly accepted as fact. Artificial intelligence can spit out entire blog posts, social media updates, and video scripts in a fraction of a second.

Oh, and there are already AI-generated influencers with big followings.

Advertisers are flocking to these avatars because, as one article I read says, "They guarantee a trouble-free experience for advertisers in an age of celebrity scandals and influencer controversies. An AI presence is engineered to perfection down to the last wisp of hair on her head."[2]

According to the founder of Virtual Humans in an interview with *Bloomberg*, "Virtual influencers are cheaper to work with than humans in the long term, are 100 percent controllable, can appear in many places at once, and, most importantly, they never age or die."[3] You can't compete. Neither can I.

The reputations of real humans (it's weird to have to define a human as "real") aren't immune from artificial intelligence either. Last week I saw a video with two of the biggest health influencers in the world, Joe Rogan and Andrew Huberman, talking back and forth with each other, recommending a penis-enlargement pill.[4]

They first spoke about the problem of confidence in young men with smaller penises, then the incredible scientific advances in the area down under, and finished by telling you where to buy the pill bottle, step-by-step, reading the domain name out loud.

As you might have already guessed, the video wasn't actually them speaking; it was a deepfake done without their permission as a social experiment *this time*. Artificial intelligence replaced their lips and voices.

Right now, a top ten health podcast isn't read by a human. The team behind Arnold Schwarzenegger's show spent months training an AI engine with his voice. This machine can now realistically read anything by him. How good is it? I'm told that the Terminator himself can't tell the difference between his voice and the machine-generated one.[5]

Arnold's using this technology for good. It's a way for him to add leverage and help more people get fit. But it's easy to see how the same technology can be used for nefarious purposes.

If his team can train an AI engine, so can anybody else. There's thousands of hours of audio and video from Arnold freely available. All it would take is for somebody with ill-intent to feed it into a machine and teach the AI his speech patterns, accent, and intonations.

What's to stop somebody else from using this same technology to promote untested supplements to impressionable young men, for example. Which, by the way, is already happening.

On February 22, 2024,[6] the first major lawsuit was filed by an influencer (Huberman) against a malicious firm called A&D Performance for using a deepfake to promote Turkesterone, Tongkat Ali, and Fadogia agrestis.

A&D Performance grabbed a clip of Huberman from the Joe Rogan podcast and used artificial intelligence to *change what he was saying.*

It's blatant. The case was dismissed on April 12, 2024, but I suspect the issue is far from over. Where will it end? These companies are offshore, making lawsuits an expensive nightmare, and by the time one of them gets taken down, fifty more will have popped up.

Ethics isn't the point. Whether or not what's happening is good or bad (or legal) is irrelevant.

The point is that there's no way to control it. Pandora's box has been opened.

The point is that there's no hope in policing it. It's moving too fast.

The point is that trust online is rapidly trending toward zero.

It's both totally reasonable and nothing new to fear technological innovation. The future is filled with unknowns, and the unknown will always be scary. Part of me wants to run away to a remote forest with a Santa Claus sack filled with guns, gold, Bitcoin, and seeds, but then I remember two things:

1. I'm Canadian, so I don't even know how to hold a gun.
2. In the 1400s, people thought printing books was the work of witches and devils.

—

Printer's Devil

The initial response to Johannes Gutenberg's printing press was . . . mixed.

Early on, his financial partner, Johann Fust, used it to sell fifty copies of the Bible and was thrown in jail on accusations of witchcraft.[7] Around the same time, the scribes of Paris feared the loss of jobs and went on strike. Printers' apprentices became known as "printers' devils." Some were murdered.

For as long as humans have invented new tools and technologies, we've worried about how they'll change us.

The Greek philosopher Socrates warned that writing would "introduce forgetfulness into the soul of those who learn it."

It was feared that telephones would tear apart the fabric of society by removing the need for people to meet face-to-face.

Radio, and later TV, was going to brainwash everyone.

Despite the initial damning response, just fifty years after the printing press was invented, the benefits were clear. Consider what the German author Sebastian Brant had to say in the year 1500:

"In our time, thanks to the talent and industry of those from the Rhine, books have emerged in lavish numbers. A book that once would've belonged only to the rich—nay, to a king—can now be seen under a modest roof. . . . There is nothing nowadays that our children . . . fail to know."[8]

"History never repeats itself," according to the French historian Voltaire, "but man always does." Throughout history, virtually every technological innovation has been met with the same response—a combination of fear of the unknown and worries surrounding job displacement.

In retrospect, the benefits are obvious. Without the printing press, you wouldn't be reading this book unless you're a king (in which case, g'day, your highness). At the time, though, Gutenberg's invention scared them shitless.

The end-of-history illusion, according to Harvard psychologist Daniel Gilbert, states that we have a tendency to simultaneously accept that things changed in the past but act like they won't change in the future.[9]

Perhaps this is why, in the moment, because the only moment we're ever in is this moment, nothing ever feels silly.

But after that moment passes and we're in a new moment, and we know now what we know, we realize how little we actually knew. It's always been this way. It will always be this way.

Whenever there's technological disruption, I think about it like it's the start of winter and it sucks outside and the sun starts going down by 5:00 p.m. You can spend your time looking out your window and being sad, or you can invite friends over, drink hot chocolate, watch terrible movies, and make fun of how lame they are. Both of these are ways to deal with the change of seasons, but one's great and the other sucks. Ultimately, our response to things out of our control is our choice.

———

McKinsey estimates that 800 million global workers could be displaced by automation and forced to find new jobs by the year 2030.[10] The great resignation is underway.

It's a good thing. Technology doesn't erase jobs, it evolves them. Innovation brings a new kind of opportunity.

Let's revisit the story that began this chapter. The Obvious Choice business model of the future is going to consist of people like me wanting to grow more veggies, hiring people like Luay—who, by now, has quit his job at a large multinational to pursue his passion of urban vegetable gardening full-time.

Luay charges $175/hour because of his unique expertise. At that rate, he only has to work an average of 11.5 hours a week to make $100,000 a year.

With his newfound spare time, he films videos, volunteers at community gardens, and has published a cookbook called *Seed to Table: A Seasonal Guide to Organically Growing, Cooking, and Preserving Food at Home*. How wonderful.

Everything's different, nothing's new. I hope you're now rightfully optimistic about the future. The logical question that follows is how to avoid getting swept up in the noise.

—

The Parade Problem

Imagine you're in Scottsdale, Arizona, for Parada Del Sol.

Thirty thousand people line the streets. It's packed; nobody can see. So, one person stands on his tiptoes. He has a good view for a few seconds.

Then everyone else stands on their tiptoes. What happens next, according to Warren Buffett, is that "your view doesn't improve, but your legs begin to hurt."

Every time tech presents a new way to share information, collect data, advertise, create content, or market in any way, it seems like an immediate winner. By standard measures, it's often better than what you were doing before: a more scalable way to reach people, an easier way to entertain, a new filter to be more attractive, or a better algorithm. The list goes on.

The problem isn't that it doesn't work; it's that it works the same for everybody.

Viewed individually, the trendy thing right now often makes sense to use. Viewed accurately as a collective, everybody's use neutralizes everybody else's.

The more people playing the same game, the harder it is for anybody to win. What initially looks like an advantage unfortunately results in us all working more, benefiting less, and burning out in an endless cycle of one-upmanship.

It's true that social media is an incredible way for you to reach people; me too.

It's also true that technology allows you to precisely target potential customers with advertisements; me too.

And, yes, it's true that artificial intelligence is a fantastic way for you to create huge amounts of content; me too.

For the earliest adopters and the most skilled, the rewards are huge. However, democratization of technology results in what can only be compared to a developing country's economy: a few super-rich elites, no middle class, and the majority of the population working hard, yet poor, hungry, and hopeless.

The Parade Problem

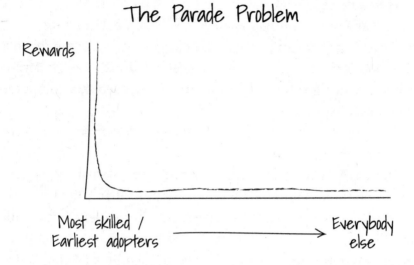

The Parade Problem demonstrates what happens whenever tech presents a new way to share information, collect data, advertise, create content, or market in any way. Viewed accurately as a collective, everybody's use neutralizes everybody else's. For the earliest adopters and the most skilled, the rewards are huge. For everybody else, rewards are minimal, irrelevant of work ethic and quality.

There's currently 254 million posts with the hashtag #photographer on Instagram. Unsurprisingly, the solution to getting bookings is not to somehow outdo them all when you produce #photographer post 254,000,001.

We all start at the same parade. The solution isn't to try to stand a bit taller. It's to find your own parade.

—

The Power of Not Making Sense

School used to be a straight path to a job—a job that can now be done by a machine.

In many ways, computers are like your brain, but better.

Anything that can be easily taught can be easily taught to a computer. Any connection that's logical has already been incorporated into an algorithm. Anything that makes sense, a computer has already learned.

Computers thrive when they're efficient. We thrive when we're strategically (in)efficient.

Get out of your bubble. Learn things the algorithm doesn't spoon-feed you in order to make connections that it can't.

Dabbling is the secret to success. Gather experiences. Talk to different people. Read widely. "It's necessary to be slightly underemployed if you are to do something significant," said James Watson, the molecular biologist who codiscovered the double helix structure of DNA. Aimless exploration is the pathway to discovery.

Attend a megachurch event, even if you're Jewish.

Get a subscription to a magazine about current events in the United Kingdom, even if you live in Canada.

Hire a boxing coach in Mexico, even if you're a 5 foot 4 pacifist who has never thrown a punch.

There's value in all of it. How? I've no clue. Over time, it'll coalesce into something uniquely human.

Maybe you'll learn about public speaking and persuasion. Or maybe you'll meet somebody somewhere who knows something about something. Or a million other maybes.

The benefits might not be immediate. For example, you might connect with a fabulous literary agent at a fitness event over a wonderful little bookstore called Friends of the Library located in her mother's hometown of Lahaina on the island of Maui where you lived for a few months a decade ago for no good reason other than it was an adventure and then she ends up representing you and your book. This book. The one you're reading. That's how I got my agent.

Or maybe nothing will come of it. That's fine, too.

I recognize that this isn't particularly useful advice. It's airy-fairy stuff. There's no framework to follow. No "steps to success." No action steps. By definition, the process is messier than the floor underneath my toddler's high chair every damn time he eats.

In many ways, machines are better, faster, and cheaper than us. You can't compete on efficiency or level of expertise. The more random things you do and learn, the more valuable you'll become. It'll feel slow, maybe even like you're wasting your time. You're not.

We put far too much emphasis on things that can be measured and not enough on stuff we can't. You don't become the Obvious Choice by doing the same thing as everybody else, just a little better. You become it by being unique.

Next, the difference between being an online entertainer and building a business.

CHAPTER 6

Figure Out What Game You're Playing Online

Good Information, Bad Advice — Hollywood Millionaires — Social Media's Goals Aren't Your Goals — Engagement Spotlights — Schmoozing Mensches — Playing the Right Game

J essica was a struggling online coach with only six paying clients.

"My issues are marketing and sales. I need a social media manager, more professional photos of myself, and more time," she said.

She had 20,600 followers on Instagram when I got her message. That's enough people to fill Madison Square Garden.

If we assume that her six clients came directly from social media, her conversion rate is 0.029 percent, or one client for every 3,433 followers. Adding free followers isn't Jessica's issue; getting paying clients is. Despite prevailing wisdom, they aren't the same thing.

—

There's an episode of *South Park* where a company of gnomes steal underwear.[1] When asked why, they lay out their master plan:

Phase 1: Steal underpants

Phase 2: ???

Phase 3: Profit

Now this might surprise you, but I'm not an experienced boxer brief thief. Still, it's obvious even to my no-underpants-stealing-self that the previous plan is missing something.

The gnomes don't know how stealing underpants leads to profit. They just started doing it one day for reasons they cannot even remember. Over time, it became habitual.

You'd think at one point a wise gnome would stand up and say, "Yo, gnomeys, we've gotta lotta underpants but no profit. Maybe takin' tighty-whiteys ain't good business after all." But they don't because, by this point, the gnomes are so used to dutifully collecting underpants that it's all they know.

Even doing the right thing badly is better than doing the wrong thing well.

The Underpants Gnomes Problem states that a lot of people are working hard at the "win the internet" game but ignoring how and if it leads to their success. It's hard to ignore social media because it's designed to be hopelessly addictive, not because it's necessarily useful.

You don't need to share every moment of your life online to be successful.

You're allowed to eat cold watermelon on a warm day without the world knowing. You don't need to take a picture of the watermelon. You don't need to think about something witty to say about it. You can eat the watermelon and enjoy the warmth of the sun on your skin as you simply live in this precious fleeting moment.

Building a business and becoming an online entertainer are different games people play—neither's better or worse, but problems arise when you conflate the two—playing by the rules of one and desiring the rewards of the other.

Good Information, Bad Advice

There was a woman onstage sharing some behind-the-scenes information about her fabulous business.

She shared four different marketing systems for three different programs. Each had its own content, emails, and paid advertising.

While impressive, I couldn't help looking around the room at the attendees' glazed-over eyes, assuming that they were thinking the same thing as me: *If I've gotta do all this just to make a living, yo, count me out.*

At this event, many of the other speakers, both men and women, had similar presentations. Something about what they were saying missed the mark.

To figure out whether good information from smart people applies to you, shift your focus away from what you see and onto what you don't.

The speakers used words like "hustle" and "sacrifice." I used to buy into those mantras. For close to a year, I worked on my online business from 9:30 p.m. to 2:00 a.m. after a full day of work. This period made me believe that if you want to one day have what others don't, you must, at one time, be willing to do what others won't.

So, what changed? Why do I think hustle culture is cringey today when, back then, I embraced it?

I got married and had kids.

"The things we respond to at twenty," the author Gabrielle Zevin wrote, "are not necessarily the same things we will respond to at forty and vice versa."

"How many of these speakers have children?" I wondered.

As it turned out, there were fifteen speakers at the event with an average age of thirty-seven. Two of them had kids. Only one of those two had built the foundation of their business with a child. The other one built their core business and then had a daughter.

So, only one of the fifteen speakers had a child as they built their business.

The guy I was sitting next to had three boys under the age of five.

Good information for one person isn't good information for everybody. A lack of children didn't render the speaker's information invalid or her success any less credible. It's simply important to consider. Obvious choices other people make might not be *your Obvious Choice*.

Missing data points often provide helpful context to figure out whether something is relevant to you. No matter how good the strategy, the "best" is not the best for all. It's totally reasonable (and very common) for good information to also be bad advice.

—

Hollywood Millionaires

In the 1920s, Hollywood became the world's film capital. For those making the pilgrimage in search of stardom, the rules of engagement were clear:

1. Low odds of success,
2. Long time horizons, and
3. Outrageous and outsized rewards for a chosen few.

Or, as the pioneering horror filmmaker George A. Romero said, "If I fail, the film industry writes me off as another statistic. If I succeed, they pay me a million bucks to fly out and fart."

There's something fantastically admirable in persevering against all odds to make dreams come true, even if it doesn't work out.

Hustling. Working for free. Waiting tables on nights and weekends to pay rent along with thousands of others who share the same dream. You know all this and still want to take your shot and go for it? Great!

The problem that I have with social media is that the rules of engagement are no longer clear. Even the biggest creators in the world are warning their followers about the siren call of easy online influence. Jimmy Donaldson (aka MrBeast) tweeted that, "It's painful to see people quit their job/drop out of school to make content full time before they're ready. For every person like me that makes it, thousands don't. Keep that in mind and be smart plz."[2]

We're tricked into thinking that this time it's different—this time the odds are somehow better—this time it won't take years of working for free for somebody else while struggling to pay our bills in the hopes that it'll all pay off, and we'll make it big, one day.

The words "influencer," "creator," and "entertainer" are synonyms. The medium has changed, but the job hasn't.

There's a wonky misconception that you have to first get famous online in order to be a success. It's the opposite. The most straightforward path to becoming influential online, if that's the goal, is to first do something meaningful. **Social media success is most often a lagging, not leading, indicator of real-world impact.**

While they're often fun to watch and good at grabbing attention, an influencer's ability to make money is limited. Admittedly it's true that a few can build huge businesses selling commoditized items like low-cost memberships, supplements, coffee, makeup, vitamin waters, hair extensions, and clothing. The ones that make it make bank. Most don't, though.

Entertainment is an outlier business: always was, and always will be.

To be clear: building a big online following is a worthwhile goal for some. All I'm pointing out is that the game of trying to become an influencer is different from the game of getting customers.

While it could contribute to business, it's not necessary for business and it's both a slower and less efficient route.

If the goal is to get famous on the internet, then following advice on how to win at social media, master the algorithm, and get as many likes as possible is a good idea. On the other hand, if the goal is to grow a business, much of that (good) information can be ignored.

Jessica, whom we met at the beginning of this chapter, thinks she's on the right path. She's convinced that the solution to her problem of getting paying clients is to do more of the same thing she's doing, just with prettier photos.

That's insane. What she's doing is clearly not working. She's playing the wrong game. I feel bad for her, though. It's not her fault. The game is rigged.

—

Social Media's Goals Aren't Your Goals

Social media platforms are for-profit enterprises. Their primary way to make money is by selling advertising.

It's a relatively simple equation: the more time people spend on their app, the richer the owners and investors of the company become. For that to happen, they needed to convince millions of people to create content every day (i.e., work for free) to feed their system. Through a combination of addictive design elements, misdirected data insights, and promises of inexplicable outlier success, they've achieved their goal.

It's one of the greatest magic tricks in modern times.

Let's revisit Jessica's example one final time. If you recall, she's been trying unsuccessfully to get customers by creating content and engaging on Instagram.

This is work, and success must be analyzed with that in mind.

If she were to calculate how much money she's made in exchange for the hundreds (maybe thousands?) of hours she's spent on Instagram, it would be far below the poverty line.

For example, if Jessica's average lifetime customer value for her six clients is $350 and she's spent a thousand hours building her business on IG, she's making $2.10 an hour. Yikes. And that doesn't include time spent actually working with clients.

Admittedly, I don't know Jessica's numbers, but I'm confident saying that the value-creation mismatch between Jessica and Instagram is outrageous.

Social media is designed to be so addicting that every time a following goes up or, gasp, doesn't go up, it can become an obsession. So much so that we lose sight of the fact that we're working tirelessly creating free content for these companies and getting negligible returns, trading our 9–5 for a 24/7.

I don't hate the platforms; nobody's evil. There's nothing wrong with social media. If the goal is to get famous, there's never been a more effective tool.

For most of us, though, what I'm describing represents a simple goal misalignment. Your goal is to spend as little time as possible on the platform and leverage it to build a business elsewhere. The platform's goal is for you to never leave the platform.

Here's a challenging question:

Do you own your online platform or does the platform own you?

At the end of the day, we cannot forget that it's our choice to use or not use social media. If you do decide to use it, you need a plan that takes into account your goals, not the goals of the social media company. I can't tell you how best to use it for your goals, but later in this chapter I'll share an example. Then, in Chapter 14, I'll provide a framework you can use to maximize the quality of the trade.

For now, think about your social media platform as a savings account. Make deposits when there's excess time and money. Think of it as an investment in the future, not a way to benefit short-term. It's okay for you to hope that it grows long-term and kicks off interest in the interim so long as you don't rely on that happening for your immediate success.

Engagement Spotlights

Goodhart's Law states, "When a measure becomes a target, it ceases to be a good measure."[3]

Superficial engagement metrics such as likes, comments, shares, and followers are all measures, not targets. Relying on them as your only insights is like playing a game with no scoreboard.

In my coaching company, we track how many inbound direct-message inquiries are received.

Bar Ape, a seasonal gelato shop, measures success by how many people show up and buy ice cream when they post about a new flavor.

Good journalists judge the quality of their writing based on how far down the page the reader made it and not how many people initially clicked (though some ratio of both is likely ideal).

"Metrics are a like a spotlight,"[4] said Jonah Berger, a marketing professor at the Wharton School and the *New York Times* best-selling author of *Contagious: Why Things Catch On*. "They shine attention on something. If that's what we want to optimize, great. But if it's not, we need to be careful because it encourages us to optimize whatever it's focused on."

What gets mismeasured gets mismanaged.

Schmoozing Mensches

As a socially awkward guy who liked to read books and lift stuff up and then put it back down ten to twelve times, give or take, walking up to pretty strangers and asking them out on a date was not something I was particularly comfortable with. *Did they already have a boyfriend?* I'd wonder.

Dating websites became popular when I was in university. It was a whole new world. For me they solved the problem of *intent*. If a girl was on there, at least I knew she was looking for *something*.

The difference between a dating website and most social media profiles is that on a dating website, intent is both specific and explicit.

If you post a pretty photo on Jdate, a dating app connecting Jewish singles, your intent is clear: you want to find a mensch to introduce to your *bubbie* and *zayde* that you can schmooze with "till the sun goes down." Post that same photo on social media and, to an outsider, what you want is anybody's guess.

There was an Instagram fitness model years back who understood this concept. I don't remember her name, but I'll never forget what she did.

First, she built up a huge following by posting overtly sexualized photos of herself. I don't judge. It's your body. You have the right to showcase it however you want.

If you do decide to build an audience this way, just know what it's good for and what it isn't.

It's easier and faster to build a bigger and more engaged audience by doing things like sexualizing your image, jumping on trends, eliciting anger, or being purposefully divisive. Sales and engagement, however, aren't the same thing.

If the way you've built an audience is inconsistent with the product or service you want to sell, you'll end up rich with likes but poor with dollars.

Almost every day, I get messaged by the men and women who own these types of accounts saying some variation of, "I have this huge audience but whenever I try to sell anything, it goes silent."

I shouldn't need to say this, but if you build a following by posting sweaty photos of boobs, butts, and abs, then I've got bad news for you: most people aren't following you for your world-renowned fitness expertise.

This one model did it differently though. She didn't sell fitness coaching. Instead, she sold an ebook. I don't remember the exact title, but it was something like *How to Date Girls Like Me.*

After I was done hating the world, I couldn't help but give her a slow clap. She knew what game she was playing. She understood the intent of her following.

Playing the Right Game

Conor O'Shea's a fitness coach looking for executive-type clients and lucrative corporate-wellness bookings. He sent me this message shortly after starting a podcast: "This is getting exciting now. I've only done four episodes but have already booked a call with a client about my coaching services before he does a podcast with me next month. I'm also in contact with Microsoft Ireland for potential corporate wellness after doing an episode with a manager there."

Conor and I spoke a few months prior. He was going to first name his show *Corporate Wellness Ireland.* I told him not to: "Tech people don't care about corporate wellness. You care about corporate wellness. Tech people care about improving their status in a world of tech people."

Conor then asked me whether it'd be better to start a show focused on Ireland instead of the city of Limerick, because Ireland has more people.

"Neither option is better or worse. They're different games, though." I said. "Ireland's what you'd create if your goal is to someday become a famous podcaster. Limerick is what you'd create if you want to use a podcast to build a targeted network and get clients right now."

He named his show the *Limerick High Performance Podcast*.

Counterintuitively, a smaller radius (or niche) is better for business development. It's direct, specific, and allows him to invite executives at local companies onto the show.

Podcasts are hard to grow. The pond is massive. Organic discovery is almost nonexistent. Becoming a famous podcaster is a notoriously hard game to play.

There's a better way to use podcasts. Leverage it to become the Obvious Choice.

"Talk to a man about himself and he will listen for hours," said British prime minister Benjamin Disraeli. Instead of cold-calling influential executives in Limerick to pitch them on corporate wellness, Conor invited them to be guests on his show. Same effort. Slight tweak. Better result.

Limerick High Performance will never be a top 100 podcast. It's never going to get a lot of downloads. That's fine. Fifty downloads from executives and heads of human resource departments in Limerick are more valuable to Conor than ten thousand random people who kind of like fitness worldwide.

Right now, Conor's working to become the Obvious Choice for fitness and corporate wellness in the Limerick tech scene. As his show grows, maybe he'll decide to expand and target all of Ireland. And then if that grows, maybe he'll decide to expand it into a general show about high performance worldwide.

Or not.

When you create content online, there's two games to choose from:

1. The "try to get famous on the internet" game
2. The "leverage online media to build your business" game

Playing the right game is simple. Do you need (or want) cash now or can you go for three to five years without making anything?

There's no wrong answer. Neither option is better or worse. They're different—with different rules of engagement, time horizons, reward mechanisms, and odds of success.

In many cases, the tools (social media, podcast, email, etc.) are the same. How you use and measure your success on them is what changes.

If you choose the "famous on the internet" game, focus on both hard and soft media skills. Study influencers, learn video editing, and uplevel on public speaking, improv comedy, and dance. Network in communities of others playing a similar game and plan for three to five years before it bears fruit.

If you choose to leverage social media as a place to build a business today, view it as a place to network and convert traffic, not generate it. Turn your platform into a place that showcases customer success, demonstrates your product or service, and answers questions. Don't compare yourself to influencers, ignore superficial engagement metrics, and instead measure metrics that relate to tangible business success.

While you can only play one well at any given time, the game can change as your goals change. What's important is that you don't expect (or rely upon) the rewards of one game, if you're playing by the rules of the other.

Now let's talk about why knowing too much about something is worse than not knowing enough.

CHAPTER 7

Remain Optimistically Ignorant

Fireball — When 1 + 1 = 10 — Leapfrog Skills — Leapfrog Learning

In many ways, knowing too much about a thing is worse than not knowing enough.

And these days we all know too much.

———

I was twenty-four years old when I self-published my first book. It's a guide for personal trainers called *Ignite the Fire*. I'd only been full-time in the gym for three years.

Nothing about writing that book at such a young age was audacious or courageous. The truth is that I knew so little about all the reasons why I shouldn't have written the book that I wrote the book.

Here's how it happened:

I carried a clipboard while I trained my clients with two items: workout programs and a blank piece of paper. On the blank piece of paper, I'd take notes. For example:

- Client complained of pain bench-pressing.
- Picked up garbage.
- Another trainer taught dead lifts wrong (dangerous?) (intervene?).
- Want to date the secretary.
- Got stopped by a member wanting to buy sessions while training a client. (What to do?)

And so on.

At night, I'd review my day by expanding on each point adding details and thoughts. In some cases, I'd call friends and ask what they'd do or have done in similar situations.

I wasn't trying to write a book. I was trying to improve by cataloging and reflecting on my day's events.

After about a year, I showed the document to my mom. It was large. About one hundred thousand words. She said it could be a book and that there was a lot of interesting material but I needed an editor.

I was a personal trainer with a kinesiology degree. I didn't know any authors, let alone any editors.

Instead of being overwhelmed by book publishing, I focused on figuring out the next step. Not on purpose. I'm creating a post-rational narrative here. The process was undoubtedly messier than how I'm describing it because, at the time, all that I knew was that editors are involved in books and bookstores have books.

So, I went to the bookstore.

There was a shelf of best-selling health and fitness books. I wrote down the names of the authors, went home, and sent cold emails to them asking for an introduction to their editor.

Almost everyone replied. Many of them made introductions. I hired Kelly James-Enger, because she told me the ideas were good but the book was not and that it needed a lot of work. I like honesty.

Once the book was edited, Kelly said now I needed a copyeditor to fix grammar, spelling, and formatting. I didn't know that was a thing, but I guess it makes sense that that's a thing.

Kelly introduced me to a copyeditor. Then I got the cover designed and the book printed. And so on.

This was 2009. There were no hybrid book-in-a-box publishers or marketplaces of reliable, outsourced help. If you wanted something done, you needed to mash together a random smattering of contractors—and those contractors could be hard to find.

When I think about that period of my life, I can best describe myself as optimistically ignorant. That's a way of saying that I was clueless but, like, in a good way.

If you wanted to do something, you figured it out. Or, you didn't, and you didn't do the thing.

Back then we were mostly blind; mostly making it up as we went. You had a binary choice to take something seriously or not. None of this wishy-washy, in-between stuff. These days, it's too easy to do a bad job with all the tips, tools, and tutorials freely available.

I know that we can't go back in time and I also know that there's more opportunity for everybody now. Still, a part of me gets nostalgic thinking about that period of my life.

Ignorance pulled me forward. I didn't know what I didn't know. But I gained confidence knowing that I could always figure out the next step. It seemed less daunting. As I solved one problem, the next became clear.

It's like when you're driving on the highway and it's pitch-black and you have your high beams on. You know you've got miles to go and there will be twists and turns, but all you can see right now is what's directly ahead of you, so you focus on that. As you continue to drive, new stretches of road light up until you approach your destination. Optimistic ignorance is kind of like that.

Ignite the Fire has sold more than 75,000 copies. I wrote it a long time ago. I'm proud of it. But I sometimes wonder whether I'd be able to do it if I were twenty-four today. Honestly, I don't think so.

Overinformed pessimism is an inevitable and unfortunate by-product of an information economy.

The reasons why somebody else is better suited than you to do the thing. Why it's hard. A bad idea. Or all the ways it could go wrong. We second-guess ourselves, not because we don't know enough, but because we know too much.

Did you know that the reason we have grassy front lawns is because, in the 1300s, medieval kings planted grass as a way to show off their wealth? According to the historian Yuval Noah Harari in his book *Homo Deus: A Brief History of Tomorrow*, grass was the perfect status symbol. It produces nothing of value, needs lots of land, and requires costly labor to maintain (this was before sprinklers and lawn mowers).

We don't need to show off our wealth with grass anymore. We have social media for that. For some reason, though, this status symbol outlasted all the monarchies that built it.

Personally, I don't have a problem with grass. But it's interesting to learn that our obsession with it is nothing more than a remnant of the past that really only exists because people kept copying one another until nobody really knew why they were growing grass, but figured there had to be a reason, so they kept doing it.

I guess what I'm saying is that copying others is an inevitable by-product of constant exposure.

If I were twenty-four and considering publishing a book today, I'd be discouraged by how many people were already saying online what I wanted to say. Not because my ideas were original before. But because now it's impossible for me not to notice that they aren't original.

If I could overcome that self-defeating narrative, I'd look up how to self-publish a book. Like Alice, I'd fall down the rabbit hole of podcast episodes, YouTube videos, and social media posts. The overwhelm would be paralyzing.

Knowing too much about a thing is often worse than not knowing enough. All the information we can access in our pockets can be a crutch rather than a support. When we become aware of all the reasons we shouldn't do something, sadly, we often don't.

Informed pessimism can't be avoided. Instead, we must learn how to overcome it. The first step is to accept that others are more qualified than you, which is totally fine.

—

Fireball

My roommate almost burned down our house in college.

He wanted to fry potatoes, so he put an inch of oil in the pan and turned the heat on. Then he smoked a joint and fell asleep.

By the time I got there, the flames were a foot high. I carried the fiery pan to the driveway and dumped water on it.

Water and oil don't mix. The water closest to the fire gets vaporized, becomes airborne, and pushes the oil away. That's a fancy way of saying that pouring a bucket of water onto a grease fire turns it into a fucking fireball. My dumb ass didn't know that at the time.

Imagine you're a firefighter. It's your first day on the job. The alarm goes off. You arrive at the house and see a pan on fire.

So, you turn off the heat source and spray a dry chemical fire extinguisher. Easy.

Once the fire's out, you tell the family that if it happens again, pour on baking soda, cover it with a metal pot, and turn off the heat, allowing it to self-suffocate from a lack of oxygen. Then you kiss a baby, pose shirtless for a calendar, and do whatever else I imagine firefighters do.

In a group of experienced firefighters, you're a newbie. Compared to them, you feel like an impostor. But you knew not to put water on a grease fire. Sure, you might get laughed at by other firefighters, but nobody you helped cared. You put out the fire.

Don't let your perceived inexperience, lack of impressive specs, or any other inadequacy related to your peers stop you.

In almost every case, the necessary methodology to solve a customer's problem isn't complicated.

How likely are you to check where your financial advisor went to school or what his grades were? I've never done it. My confidence in his ability has nothing to do with how well he did as a business student.

Did you ever wonder why some nutrition coaches do very well while others barely make a living? Successful nutrition coaches don't necessarily know more about the Krebs cycle than other nutrition coaches. Most people just need to eat a bit more protein and a lot less crap.

The Total Classic Original Blender from Blendtec has a "powerful 1560 watt motor." A blender from another company, Ninja, only has a 900-watt motor. What does that mean? I've no idea. I have, however, owned both, and both make an equally good smoothie.

Here's a challenging question: Are you learning because it will meaningfully affect your customer's outcome? Or are you learning because it's personally interesting to you?

Ambitious people often struggle because they're too narrowly focused on their field, obsessing over minute details irrelevant to the customer. The Obvious Choice doesn't rise above because they know more than others in their field; they rise because they see opportunities that others don't.

Getting better at things we're already good at feels good. It's comfortable. In many ways, though, it's selfish.

The selfless approach is to recognize when you're good enough to solve the core problem, freeing yourself up to add complementary skills that improve the potency of your industry expertise.

This isn't permission to coast in your profession. Always strive to learn and improve. Instead, it's an introduction to a more important conversation—one that appreciates that not all personal development is equal.

———

When 1 + 1 = 10

Industry-specific knowledge reaches the point of diminishing returns rather quickly. (I'm ignoring the outlier cases that involve the best in the world.)

Take me, for example. I was a highly successful personal trainer with a basically okay knowledge of fitness and a decent understanding of psychology.

But what I also had that most people in my industry didn't was a mediocre ability to write and sell.

If you were to assess my talent in any of those things independent of one another, I'd be low- to mid-tier. The combination of skills was rare and, as a result, my market value increased dramatically.

Flash-forward to today and I'd consider myself to be a good writer who also happens to have a solid all-around business background, decent understanding of psychology, and mediocre skill sets in money management, public speaking, and product development. There are better writers. More experienced businesspeople. And better psychologists.

People don't buy what you do; they buy into the belief that you can help them solve their problem.

Not only that, the people buying from you are rarely in your industry. As a result, they don't share your obsession over your expertise. It's not an area you can expect to connect with them on. The way to connect with them is on something that they're interested in. You don't know what that is. Therefore, the more things you're knowledgeable on and interested in, the better your chance of connecting uniquely.

"If you want to be interesting, be interested. If you want to be fascinating, be fascinated," wrote Chet Holmes in *The Ultimate Sales Machine*.

Improving a good enough industry skill set results in small, incremental benefits. Call it 1 + 1 = 2. When you begin adding outside skills, growth becomes exponential. 1 + 1 doesn't equal 2 anymore; it equals 10. That's obviously not an accurate calculation, but it's a useful simplification. "Successwise," wrote the cartoonist Scott Adams in his book *How to Fail at Almost Everything and Still Win Big*, "you're better off being good at two complementary skills than being excellent at one."

The Obvious Choice stands out by making connections when others don't. As a result, they see opportunities others won't.

Your value rarely relies on expertise, but in range.

You can try very hard to become truly great at one thing. Or you can combine multiple skills. Both strategies work. The advantages of combining skills is that they can be learned quickly, because none of them need to be high-level or depend on extraordinary talent. The versatility they bring can also help you adapt to an evolving world.

Not all skills are created equal. Juggling knives is cool. So is domesticating feral kittens. But those won't help you much. Unless you do them at the same time. I'd pay to watch that.

Let's first talk about which skills are the most valuable to learn. Then the best way to learn them.

Leapfrog Skills

Leapfrog Skills are timeless. Advancements in technology might make them easier to implement but won't render them less valuable.

Leapfrog Skills are also transferable. They can be combined with any industry expertise to make you more valuable. With them, you'll have an advantage in any entrepreneurial venture or become indispensable to your employer, allowing you to command a higher salary. If you change industries, you'll take them with you.

These are the top five Leapfrog Skills.

1. **Business writing:** Get to the point. Hook the reader. Tell a story. Write simply. Offer an actionable takeaway.
2. **Behavioral psychology:** Recognize, navigate, and take ethical advantage of the major cognitive biases.
3. **Conversation:** Ask the types of questions that encourage others to talk about themselves.
4. **Sales:** You get what you want by helping others get what they want.
5. **Wealth management:** Make money with money. With patience, even a little bit of money is enough money to make meaningful money.

The following is a good guideline for how the most successful people in their fields focus their professional development over time.

- Year 1: 75 percent industry skills / 25 percent Leapfrog Skills
- Year 2: 50 percent industry skills / 50 percent Leapfrog Skills
- Year 3 onward: 25 percent industry skills / 75 percent Leapfrog Skills

Industries have different baseline levels of knowledge required for results. Your ratio might be different, but even if it is, it's probably not by much.

You can access a curated list of recommended resources, books, and podcasts to get better at each Leapfrog Skill at www.JonathanGoodman.com/Leapfrog.

—

Leapfrog Learning

Focus is the key to skill acquisition in a world determined to distract us. Nothing's new about that advice. You hear it all the time. Focus more. The art of focus. "The secret to success is to be more focused," they say. Well, how do you *decide* on your focus? Then, how do you *stay* focused?

Leapfrog Learning has two parts:

1. Sixty-day focused sprints
2. Teach

A timeless success principle for fitness and personal development is that if you put in the dedicated work to build strength and resilience *one time*, you can put up with more *over time*.

The body finds comfort and stability around a homeostatic set point. Once it's set, there's a bit of fluctuation but not much. If you're trying to meaningfully improve your fitness, the goal of training is to reset your body's "normal" to a higher level of functioning. This is best done through relatively short (eight to twelve weeks) intense periods of dedicated, consistent, and reliably progressive intensity.

I've grossly oversimplified the physiological process. My kinesiologist friends are going to have a *kanipshit*. But that's as sciency as I want to get. It'll do.

Leapfrog Learning takes the same homeostatic set point principle from physiology and applies it to skill acquisition. The best way to stack skills is to choose one at a time and focus for sixty days of dedicated effort.

Why sixty days?

It's long enough to develop a mediocre level of skill yet short enough to feel doable.

Once you learn a skill, having it becomes your new normal. Like building muscles or riding a bike, if you don't use it for a while it'll get rusty but come back quickly.

Now onto the second part of Leapfrog Learning: teaching it.

A lot of work these days includes listening and reading. That's where most people stop.

Teaching helps you retain more than 90 percent of what you're learning as opposed to listening and reading, which generally sits around 20 percent knowledge retention rates. These numbers aren't scientific. Whether they're technically accurate or not isn't as important as the pattern: **Teaching is the best way to learn and retain what you learn.**

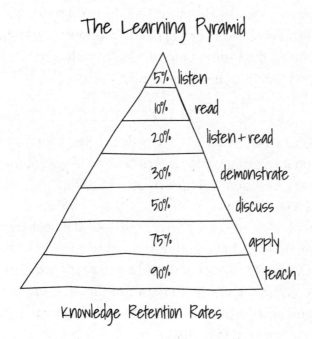

The Learning Pyramid

- 5% listen
- 10% read
- 20% listen + read
- 30% demonstrate
- 50% discuss
- 75% apply
- 90% teach

Knowledge Retention Rates

Here's three examples of Leapfrog Learning:

Get better at social media by choosing one platform to master, listening to podcasts, reading blog posts, and studying the top accounts. After sixty days, build a slide deck, invite three friends over, feed them pizza (without pineapple—pineapple on pizza is gross), and present what you've learned.

Build your personal wealth management philosophy by studying topics like greed and envy, interviewing financial advisors, reading books about investing, and listening to case studies where knowledgeable people share honestly what they do with their own money. After sixty days, teach a loved one about your philosophy or record a podcast episode about it.[1]

Figure out what to do about artificial intelligence by reading books and listening to experts speak about how it's going to redefine job roles in the future. Once done, compile a report for your industry and send it to five colleagues.[2]

———

What's useful about focus is that a little bit goes a long way. Every time you do a leapfrog period, you'll find yourself not just a little bit ahead of where you were previously, but a lot.

There's a few key lessons we can pull out here . . .

The first is that you can always figure out the next step.

The second is that single-industry knowledge reaches a point of diminishing returns rather quickly, and so it's totally okay that others in your field know more than you. Good, even.

The third is that combining mediocre skill sets in multiple areas has exponential benefits.

My decision to self-publish a book as a twenty-four-year-old personal trainer sent me down a road, blind as a bat, with no idea where I was heading.

Writing forced me to become a better writer. Then I had to sell the book, which led to advertising, copywriting, marketing, and sales. Public speaking followed, along with finance and wealth generation, improving my value and income with every new skill.

I developed the Leapfrog Learning framework to give me permission to go all-in for a short period, get good enough at a thing, recognize the point of diminishing returns, and confidently move on to the next.

Successwise, it's best to become an expert at one thing and merely proficient at many complementary things.

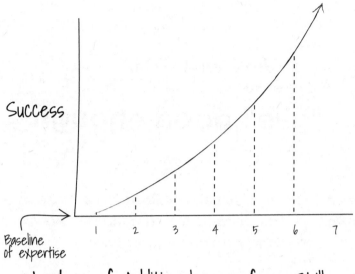

Success

Baseline
of expertise

1   2   3   4   5   6   7

Number of Additional Leapfrog Skills

With each Leapfrog Skill you add to your baseline of expertise,
your level of success improves exponentially.

It's okay to not know it all. Accept that the road ahead is pitch-black. Let your progress pull you forward, lighting the way as you go.

Next, an appreciation that one of the hardest things to do is to be consistently good long enough for it to pay off.

CHAPTER 8

"g-e" good enough

Lazy, Clever Germans — Bringing a Knife to a Gunfight — The Second Marshmallow — Wayfinding — Finding Your "Good Enough"

Usain Bolt ate a thousand McDonald's chicken nuggets on his way to winning three gold medals over ten days at the 2008 Olympics in Beijing.

What sounds insane makes total sense. He needed protein and couldn't afford to get sick. "They were the only food I could properly trust which wouldn't affect my stomach," wrote Bolt in his memoir *The Fastest Man Alive.*

Eliminating even the smallest bit of catastrophic risk is often worth sacrificing optimization.

Good enough, repeatedly, is how you get great.

—

If you go to the gym and do the most intense workout in the world, you'll look in the mirror after and see . . . nothing.

Then if you go back the next day and do another intense work-out, you'll look in the mirror and see . . . nothing.

Do a decent workout for long enough, however, and you'll wake up one day in the future transformed.

How long will it take? I've no idea. That's the hard part.

Simon Sinek describes the difference between intensity and consistency like this:

Intensity is like going to the dentist—it's fixed in time, we know exactly what date we're going, we know how long we're going to be there, . . . and we know that when we come out our teeth will feel smooth and look pearly. . . . But if that's all we do, all of our teeth will fall out.

In other words, intensity is not enough.

So, we're also supposed to brush our teeth twice a day for two minutes in the morning and two minutes in the evening.

What does brushing our teeth do for two minutes?

Nothing. It does absolutely nothing. Unless you do it Every. Single. Day. Can you leave out a day? Sure. How many days can you leave out? I don't really know. How many times do you have to brush your teeth before it works? I don't know that either.[1]

Good workout advice is to always leave one or two reps in reserve.

To not complete every set at your full capacity.

To stay below your maximum threshold.

To leave some gas in the tank.

If you want to get into great shape, it's best to avoid maximum effort the majority of the time and instead focus on stacking small exercise wins *over time*.

In addition to the obvious benefits of injury avoidance, improved recovery, and motivation, the 85 percent rule, popularized by the eight-time gold medalist sprinter Carl Lewis, actually improves performance in both fitness and work. Dan Go, a popular fitness coach and writer, shared on Twitter: "Going at 85 percent is a mindset about relaxation and performing at a high level while being in flow. It's about pacing, form, and finishing. At 85 percent, you're not striving or straining by operating at the very limit of your ability. You have room to think, focus, and adapt."[2]

"Excellence is mundane," wrote the sociologist Daniel Chambliss. "Excellence is accomplished through the doing of actions, ordinary in themselves, performed consistently and carefully, habitualized, compounded together, added up over time."

A mystery is information nobody knows. A secret is concealed knowledge. Books and podcasts tend to mystify excellence. With success, according to Chambliss, "There is no secret: there is only the doing of all those little things, each one done correctly, time and again, until excellence in every detail becomes a firmly ingrained habit, an ordinary part of one's everyday life."[3]

When the three-time Olympic gold medal–winning swimmer Mary Meagher was asked what the public least understood about her sport, she said, "People don't know how ordinary success is."[4]

Becoming elite is a remarkably dull process.

The podcaster Steph Smith wrote: "In reality, so long as you 1) choose your daily actions wisely, and 2) consistently execute over time, good things will reliably happen. . . . To be clear, consistency isn't necessarily the easiest way to success, but one that can be achieved with a higher level of certainty."[5]

———

We were living in a condo that overlooked the ocean in the Dominican Republic. For a month, we'd watch the crashing waves. Then, one day, the tide picked up. Within twenty-four hours, we were evacuated as the ocean ripped apart the high-end resort.

"A fad is a wave in the ocean, and a trend is the tide," wrote Al Ries and Jack Trout in *The 22 Immutable Laws of Marketing*. "A fad gets a lot of hype, and a trend gets very little. Like a wave, a fad is very visible, but it goes up and down in a big hurry. Like the tide, a trend is almost invisible, but it's very powerful over the long term."

"Never mistake a clear view for a short distance," advised Stanford professor Paul Saffo.[6] Superfluous and superficial tactics get undue attention. It's true that success leaves clues. But what's visible is like an iceberg, floating with one-seventh of its bulk above water. The work that really matters is invisible to the eye.

Be wary of advice that has the shelf life of a brown banana. Instead, categorize information as either permanent or expiring. Ask yourself, "In five years, will this still work?" Expiring advice isn't necessarily bad. It does, however, tend to distract us.

The hard part isn't choosing your actions; it's sticking with them. First, a quick story about a German general who was forced into retirement for opposing Hitler in 1934.[7] Then, some encouragement to maintain a steady pace below your maximum threshold. And finally, a process for finding your good enough. Let's dig in.

Lazy, Clever Germans

General Kurt von Hammerstein-Equord was a German officer famous for two things: opposing Hitler and how he categorized officers.

According to von Hammerstein, every officer possesses at least two of the following qualities: clever, lazy, stupid, and industrious.[8]

One of the hardest things to do is to be consistently good long enough for it to pay off. Impactful daily efforts can be quite small when they're focused. A few examples:

If you're a thought leader, writing five hundred words a day will take you thirty minutes to an hour. Do that for three and a half months, and you'll have the first draft of a fifty-thousand-word book.

If you want to get into shape, three hours of exercise a week is enough to reduce your risk of heart disease, depression, weight gain, diabetes, certain types of cancers, and premature death. That's 1.8 percent of your time.

If you work in real estate, ten personal messages every weekday to touch base with leads adds up to 2,600 people you've given personal attention to every year.

Impactful tasks take a small percentage of the time in every field. Most of the rest of that time is filled with notifications, interruptions, or things we're not sure we should do but think maybe we should do for reasons we cannot explain.

Busyness is a punishment imposed on people for indiscriminate thinking. For neglecting to make the few critically important decisions. For lacking the fortitude to stick with a plan. And sticking to a plan is challenging. For example:

- It's hard to stick to a routine of writing five hundred words a day.
- It's easy to jump from trend to trend, focusing on whatever social media short-form content is in vogue.

- It's hard to call ten leads every day to touch base.

- It's easy to buy into some newfangled software tool that measures a small and largely inconsequential metric.

- It's hard to be okay with knowing enough to take action.
- It's easy to listen to "just one more podcast," hoping that it holds the secret you've been missing.

General Hammerstein-Equord knew that hard work is often misdirected. Under his command, the lazy-yet-clever officers got the best positions and the stupid-yet-hardworking ones got fired. All others were kept on and given manual labor roles.

Smart people achieve more by doing less, better. By avoiding work not worth doing.

The *New Yorker* essayist Tim Kreider once wrote that he was the laziest ambitious person that he knew.[9] I love that.

—

Bringing a Knife to a Gun Fight

"It's easy to get bogged down searching for the optimal plan for change: The fastest way to lose weight, the best program to build muscle, the perfect idea for a side hustle," wrote James Clear. He then added that "the only way to become excellent is to be endlessly fascinated by doing the same thing over and over. You have to fall in love with boredom."

What a wonderful idea in theory.

The faulty assumption is that it's possible to seek boredom. Social media, email, shopping, video games, news, television, and even online dating are all too well-designed. The psychological challenge is too great. "It's like bringing a knife to a gunfight," said Tim Ferris.[10] You can't rely on self-control or discipline.

Don't seek boredom. Seek the freeing feeling that comes when you're content with your rhythm.

One simple way to achieve this sort of contentment is to never log on to the internet. For most of us, that isn't realistic.

Another way is to add more technology like website blockers, time trackers, and productivity apps that cover up the effects their sister companies have created.

Then there's the slew of focus drugs, some legal and some not.

So far, the only options, it seems, are to remove ourselves from society, layer on more tech as a Band-Aid, or use brain-chemistry-altering drugs. Sounds awful.

And yet, our primitive brains are underequipped for navigating an evolved world. We can't swap them out for updated models. Instead, we need to work with what we've got. For me, a new insight from an old psychological experiment held the key.

—

The Second Marshmallow

The Stanford marshmallow experiment is a study on delayed gratification from 1972.[11] Kids were given a marshmallow and told to wait. If they didn't eat it by the time the experimenter got back, they got a second marshmallow.

Then the kids were followed up with for decades. The ones who delayed gratification—the ones who didn't immediately shove the marshmallow in their face—were more successful later in life.

While the predictive power of the specific study has been questioned, the idea that delaying gratification—doing the hard work today and putting off the reward in the hopes that it'll benefit you later—will result in later success is hard to argue.[12]

We had Chinese hot pot dinner at my mother-in-law's (we call her Poh Poh) condo the night before I wrote this section. Poh Poh bought marshmallows to roast. The bag had both pink and white ones. I don't understand why they make pink marshmallows;

they're weird. White marshmallows, on the other hand, are a gift sent from the heavens.

Before dinner my son and I had "just one." I was a responsible father. He only had one. I was not, however, a responsible human: I ate all the white ones. *All of them.*

Here's my problem with the 1972 study: I would've eaten that marshmallow before the researcher even stood up. I'm hopelessly addicted to immediacy. Delayed gratification sounds nice, but it just ain't me. My lizard brain's too unevolved for it. So, what? Am I screwed?

Most people are like me. We need ongoing rewards and attaboys and thumbs-ups. Big audacious goals aren't motivating. They're too far away. I need positive reinforcement *now*. The process, therefore, must become both the focus and the reward.

You've heard this before, I know. "Fall in love with the process" is advice that sells a lot of self-help books. Admittedly, it's hard. The best advice I've ever gotten that I've never followed is to enjoy the journey.

Sometimes, though, I'm able to find ounces of enjoyment in the day-to-day mundanity. With the admission that I'm not perfect, I'll share with you a few things that I do when I'm doing this right and that I start doing again when I catch myself messing this up.

The first is to fail better, faster.

Failure's like a bee sting. Before you get stung, you're told it hurts but you don't know how much. It's scary. The unknown always is. And, of course, getting stung hurts. But then it's over, and you realize that it wasn't a big deal and life goes on and so you aren't as scared of it happening the next time. Failure's like that. The more it happens, the less afraid of it you become.

The second is to break up a large task into small parts and build in mini rewards for process wins.

A few examples:

- **Post more often on social media** by texting a friend a thumbs-up emoji whenever you've done it.
- **Write your book by breaking it up into sections of three hundred to seven hundred words.** Put the title for each section on a cue card. Once finished, flip that cue card face down on the left side of your computer.
- **Perform your daily sales calls by keeping twenty-five paper clips on your desk.** Every time you make a call, drop one paper clip in a cup.

Designing a small reward, ideally both visual and tactile, as a measurement of small progress representative of a bigger thing might help keep you going long enough to achieve something great.

———

Wayfinding

When the author Neil Gaiman sits down to write, he gives himself an option: write or not write.

"What I love about that is I'm giving myself permission to write or not write, but writing is actually more interesting than doing nothing after a while. You sit there and you've been staring out the window now for five minutes, and it kind of loses its charm. You're going, 'Well, actually, let's all write something,'" Gaiman said.[13]

He later added: "You don't have to write. You have permission to not write. But you don't have permission to do anything else."

A series of studies at Boston University tested the difference between the words "I don't" and "I can't."[14]

One hundred twenty people were split into two groups. Members of one group told themselves, "*I don't* eat candy," and the others told themselves, "*I can't* eat candy." Then they were offered a chocolate bar.

The "I can't" group ate the bar 61 percent of the time. The "I don't" group ate it 36 percent of the time.

A 25 percent difference in self-control resulted from this subtle change of words. Why? Because "I can't" is a restriction, not a choice. "I don't," on the other hand, retains your sense of power and personal agency.

I'm writing a book now. This book. It's a big project. The release date is more than a year away. I've already been working on it for a year and a half. The goal to release this book is simply too big and too far away to be motivating.

Goals are intense, fleeting, and binary.

You either achieve a goal or you don't. If you don't, you've failed. If you do, you'll be rewarded with fleeting momentary pleasure.

After briefly celebrating climbing the mountain, you'll feel empty because the only thing that was giving you purpose is now gone. The only way to get that feeling back is to declare another goal, setting you up for a cycle of perpetual misery, always striving to get *there*, never being *here*.

The British writer Alan Watts observed that we're trained to have this misguided obsession with goals from a young age:

As a child, you are sent to nursery school. In nursery school, they say you are getting ready to go on to kindergarten. And then first grade is coming up and second grade and third grade. . . . In high school, they tell you you're getting ready for college. And in college you're getting ready to go out into the business world. . . . [People are] like donkeys running after carrots that are hanging in front of their faces from sticks attached to their own collars. They are never here. They never get there. They are never alive.

Perhaps this is why I hated school but loved education.

I'll do everything in my power to make this book a success. But I'm also aware that I can't control the outcome. And so, if it doesn't succeed, I'll be sad, and then I'll move on and begin the next. And if it does succeed, I'll be happy, and then I'll move on and begin the next. So long as I stick to this plan, success is guaranteed. How long will it take? I've no idea. Will I recognize when I've succeeded? Unlikely.

And so, the book's release isn't a goal. It's more a waypoint that acts like a beacon, guiding my daily actions. Most mornings at 5:00 a.m., I sit down at my kitchen table intending to write for two hours. Some days I don't. Some days I stare out the window. But I'm okay with that because I've given myself two choices: write, or do nothing.

Conventional wisdom suggests that you have to set goals. But if you study successful people, you'll discover that most don't do it. Maybe they started with goal setting, but they never attribute their success to their goals—they attribute it to their systems.

Systems are consistent, reliable, and fluid.

System-oriented thinking views goals as beacons—something to aim toward. They provide direction, pulling you forward in the correct, broad direction.

Achievements are best viewed as waypoints, part of a greater journey, and not endpoints, the end of one journey and beginning of another.

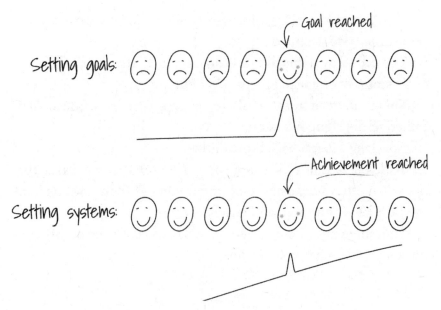

Setting goals:

Goal reached

Setting systems:

Achievement reached

If your goal is the only thing giving you purpose, its rewards are short-lived. The only way to get back the positive feeling is to set another goal. What happens next is an unfortunate cycle of momentary joy followed by perpetual misery. System setting, on the other hand, provides for more ongoing and balanced enjoyment.

The key thing about systems is that they focus on a set of behaviors, not outcomes, and anticipate ups and downs, because nobody is perfect and we have to account for that.

If you're in business, your goal might be to make more money. Your system might be to have a minimum of ten sales conversations a day. Whether or not you make a sale that day isn't as important as performing the calls, because if you perform the calls, good things will happen.

If you're in fitness, your goal might be to get in shape. Your system might be as simple as putting your workout clothing on. Whether or not you work out that day isn't as important as putting your clothing on because, most days, if you put your workout clothes on, you're going to exercise. But if you don't, that's fine. Because some days you won't be feeling it.

If you're in a relationship, your goal isn't to be married. It's to be a supportive partner.

The only way to become the noun is to do the verb, reliably.

Systems over goals. Process over outcome.

Then, sales call by sales call, rep by rep, word by word, you'll be pulled in the right direction.

How long will it take? I don't know.

Will you recognize it when you get there? Unlikely. But that doesn't matter, because the moment you get there, it'll become the new here and there will be a new there, anyway.

Still, there are a lot of different things you could be doing. How do you decide what to focus on?

Finding Your "Good Enough"

First, dedicate time for a series of rapid tests. Experiment. Study yourself.

Write a list of everything that you feel you should be doing (knowing that you can only choose one at the end). Then, every one or two weeks, try out one at a time.

For example, let's say you choose podcasting as one of your tests. For two weeks, immerse yourself by recording a podcast every day and consuming information only about podcasts.

Your testing cycles should be brief, so that you can run through a lot of experiments quickly. They won't be long enough to get any results. That's fine. It's not results that you're after, it's confidence in the process.

Maybe after podcasts, you'll try networking with local businesses, or YouTube, or knocking on doors, or writing blog posts. After each test, answer three questions:

1. Did I enjoy this?

2. Do I feel I could get good at this?
3. If I were to continue this for a year, would I be in a better place than I am now?

Once you've answered yes to all three questions, you're done. You've found what's right for you—your thing. Let your "good" then guide your development, focused on four elements: soft skills, technical know-how, network, and execution.

For example, let's say you chose to create videos for YouTube.

- **Soft skills:** Join a local improv group to level up your presentation, humor, and storytelling.
- **Technical know-how:** Learn best practices for video production, thumbnail creation, and converting viewers to customers.
- **Network:** Organize a local group of aspiring video creators. Once done, invite well-known YouTubers to share with your up-and-comer group.
- **Execution:** Publish a weekly video.

A while back I heard somebody give the advice to figure out what you're good at without trying, then try.

I like that.

———

It was the final day of one of those marketing events where every guy seemed to be wearing standard marketing-guy apparel: dark blue jeans, white V-neck, blazer, and a pre-faded leather satchel from the Banana Republic.

The final speaker was Michael Gerber, author of *The E-Myth Revisited*, with more than 5 million copies sold. He was different: big smile, gray beard, straw hat, and no slides.

Silent for a few seconds, he took in the crowd and said: "Now, I just got here so didn't see any of the other speakers but can guess what they did. I bet they all had some nice-looking PowerPoint and a fancy acronym outlining a system that'll solve all your problems and that you can learn more about if you buy their book in the lobby."

I sat forward in my chair. Gerber continued:

"I don't have any of those things. The truth is that I'm just making it up as I go; always have. *Don't you realize you can, too?*"

——

There might be a Capital B "Best" way to do something. Never forget that there are seemingly infinite lowercase "g–e" good enough ways that'll also work just fine.

What you choose to do doesn't have to be the best. You'll never know if it is, anyway. What's important is that it's *good enough*. Once you've found your good enough, stop looking. Sure, there might be *better*. But the compounding only begins when you start and stops when you change or quit.

Find your good, close the book, and execute. And, yeah, you can make it up as you go. I sure as heck am.

Now it's time for you to learn how to let your geek flag fly.

PART 2

Becoming the
Obvious Choice

CHAPTER 9

Let Your Geek Flag Fly

What's My Age Again? — Ken Griffey Jr. — The Algorithm — SNASA — Can They Pay? — Your 1 Percent Uniqueness Factor

H aving a vision for your business is like reading Twitter your entire life and then discovering that there's such a thing as books. The world stops being scary and overwhelming and starts to make sense.

Anxiety and overwhelm don't result from the amount of work you have to do; they're the result of not knowing whether the work you're doing is making any damn difference.

Your competitive advantage is that you're unique and special and weird. We all are.

———

Ben Mudge got popular online because of his long hair and resemblance to Thor. He was good at creating content but found it difficult to make sales despite having more than a hundred thousand followers.

Nothing about him stood out. Even with a big audience, he was yet another muscular dude who made nice videos about exercise on the internet. As a result, he was the okay choice for a lot of people and not the Obvious Choice for any.

He was playing it safe, hiding his true self. You'd never know it from his videos, but behind closed doors, Ben's a certified dork *obsessed* with a miniature fantasy game called *Warhammer*.

"Be authentic" is advice you hear all the time. "Be true to yourself," they say.

It's not authenticity you need. It's trusting that your authentic self is enough.

Take what you do seriously, but don't take yourself too seriously. Archaic industry norms are designed to bring everybody to the middle—the safe spot—where nobody disrupts the natural order. Customers don't buy from industries; they buy from humans. Professionalism is a lie that needs to die.

The best way to become the Obvious Choice online is to share a nerdy obsession—an uncommon commonality—with a subset of people. Being unique and special and weird are your competitive advantage.

Lambert's Cafe is a restaurant where the staff throw food at the customers. Their website is literally throwedrolls.com. The diner has become a destination. Buses line up at their door.

Cards Against Humanity runs anti-sale, satirical Black Friday promotions as a statement opposing consumerism. In 2014, they sold literal poop (sterilized bull feces) for $6 each. More than thirty thousand people bought it. They donated the profits to charity.[1]

The Sports Bra is a bar that only shows women's sports.[2] It raised $105,135 on Kickstarter and did its first million dollars in revenue within eight months of opening.[3]

And Ben, well, Ben's a muscular guy from Belfast who plays a tabletop fantasy battle game called *Warhammer*.

Warhammer's an expensive hobby that requires disposable income. The majority of players are men and many of them have difficulties in social scenarios. As a socially awkward man myself, believe me when I tell you how much getting all jacked and muscular and stuff helps with the, *ahem*, ladyfolk.

Women tell me that they don't care much about big biceps; they're attracted to confidence. But guys like me are stupid and don't get it. So, we want muscular arms and think that girls like them and that gives us confidence, which girls actually do like. I guess what I'm saying is that, in a roundabout way, muscular arms for socially awkward guys like me actually helps get girls. It's weird—took me a while to figure this all out.

Warhammer players have money and are motivated to get into shape. As a result, they're a great market for physique training. No longer embarrassed by his secret hobby and armed with clarity around what he wanted to sell, who the customers were, and what they wanted, Ben had to figure out the next step: *Where am I going to find them?*

David Nordquist runs the biggest YouTube channel for *Warhammer* called *MiniWarGaming* with more than half a million subscribers. Ben's a fan and sent him a message saying he was going to be in the area of his studio and could he drop by. Dave said yes, and Ben booked a flight so he'd actually be in the area (he lives in Ireland while Dave is in Canada).

In addition to Ben building his own *Warhammer* audience, he's putting Dave through a documented physique transformation.

For example, in a video published on August 6, 2023, called "I Lost 40 Pounds for a *Warhammer*-Inspired Movie Role," Dave said, "Ben Mudge is a dude who looks like Thor, okay. He's a bodybuilder, fitness coach, and he plays *Warhammer* so, . . . Perfect combination, right?"[4]

"Different is better than better," according to Sally Hogshead in her book *How the World Sees You.* "Different doesn't try to turn you into something else. Different allows you to highlight the singular traits you already have within you. You aren't necessarily better than your competition. But you are already different."

Don't aim to be the best; aim to be the only.

For years, Ben was playing the physique coaching game on hard mode, demonstrating exercises online, creating undifferentiated content, and wondering why more people weren't buying. He was good at it and built a large following. The magic happened—his path became clear—once he let his geek flag fly.

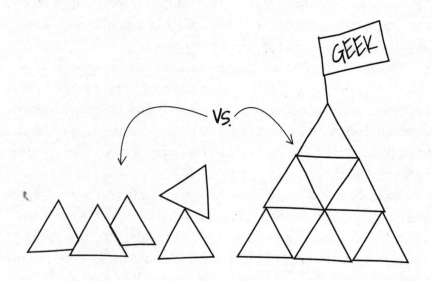

We all have enough foundational pieces. The secret
is to build your foundation on what makes you unique.

What's My Age Again?

At thirty-six years old, I decided that I didn't want to act my age and bought tickets to go to my first electronic dance music (EDM) festival called VELD with my wife. The daytime DJs were great. We danced like fools.

Nighttime hit and the crowds arrived. Forty thousand scream-ing EDM fans packed into the field as the famous DJ Martin Garrix took the stage.

The noise from the speakers mixed with the screaming dancers all around us was deafening. If Alison and I wanted to speak, I'd have to yell into her ear. I could have screamed at the top of my lungs and nobody else would have heard what I said.

A whisper on a quiet night stands out, but if you're in the mid-dle of a mosh pit at an EDM festival, nobody hears even the loudest scream.

You become the Obvious Choice by finding the quiet space, not yelling louder in an already noisy place.

The internet's full of quiet spaces. Finding them isn't hard. To do it, you've gotta accept that you're probably weird, and there are others who are weird in that same way and that's kinda cool.

We left VELD early and got home by 10:30 p.m. It was a late night for these two parents. I promise to continue to try to not act my age, though I don't like my odds.

———

Ken Griffey Jr.

Brian Pirrip was making travel television shows with China. Then COVID-19 destroyed everything he had built for ten years.

To pass the time, he started sharing about his nerdy obsession—baseball cards.

It began with a video posted to a new TikTok account about the 1986 Donruss Jose Canseco rookie card he had at his desk. Thirty-seven thousand people watched it. He did another one the next day about Ken Griffey Jr.'s Upper Deck rookie card. A hundred thousand people watched it in the first twenty-four hours.

"It's amazing how shameful I felt about sports cards," said Brian. "I mean, this has been a huge hobby of mine since I was a kid. But there was this feeling that, as a grown man, I shouldn't be going and buying trading cards—that it's something the kids do. Once I started talking about it these past two years, I realized that it's a normal thing. There's a lot of dudes doing this."

I'm one of those dudes. Like Brian, I'm irrationally passionate about baseball cards.

Specifically, I'm obsessed with my Ken Griffey Jr. rookie cards and could geek out on obscure facts about the junk wax era of the nineties for hours. For example, Griffey's famous Upper Deck rookie was doctored. It's an airbrushed photo of him in his minor league San Bernardino uniform. The company rushed to be the first to release his rookie card. He hadn't ever worn a Seattle Mariners jersey at the time.[5]

Brian's my favorite person to follow on the internet.

Behind whom to marry and where to live, deciding what to do for work is the most important decision you'll ever make.

You have two options: choose a market you're irrationally obsessed with or find a way to add your weirdness into what you already do.

Next, make sure that others share your obsession. In his book *Expert Secrets*, Russell Brunson suggests four things that must exist in obsessed markets:

1. **Communities**—Are there groups, YouTube accounts, blogs, and podcasts already dedicated to it?
2. **Vocabulary**—Does the market have its own special language?
3. **Events**—Does it have events like conferences, summits, seminars, or shows?
4. **Other experts**—Are there other experts and gurus in the market?

"What usually ends up happening with most things we feel shame about in life is that once we start telling people about it and being our authentic self, people love it!" said Brian.

Irrational obsession results in boundless energy.

Brian spent three hundred nights in a Marriott Hotel in 2023. He has so much fun talking to other collectors and card shop owners that he can't not do it. He attends every show and visits every shop, sharing the journey on social media. As a result, Brian's gained both a loyal online following and a large Rolodex of sports card collectors.

You hear the advice to surround yourself with good people in order to be successful all the time. That's good advice. But it's not just good people you need. It's *your* good people.

"It's not just the topic you're geeking out on every day," said Brian. "It's who you're geeking out with." The quality of your relationships dictates the quality of your life.

When you're personally obsessed about a thing, you understand it in ways others don't. What aspects of the market frustrate you? "Why hasn't somebody built a better widget for this?" If it bothers you, it bothers other people like you, too.

In Brian's case, what bothers him is the outdated way that cards are displayed and protected.

In 2022, for example, a 1952 Topps Mickey Mantle card sold at auction for $12.6 million.[6] The treasure was displayed in an ugly plastic case with no ultraviolet light protection. To collectors, cards are art pieces. Yet they're stored in junky plastic and degrade over time if exposed to light.

Brian scratched his own itch and launched the M1NT case—the first-ever innovation of its kind in sports card collecting's 140-year history.

During his travels, Brian shares prototypes of his M1NT case with card shop owners, trade show sellers, and podcasters. The presale list is thousands of names long.

But it's not just collectors. Professional athletes are on social media, too. And many of them are fans of Brian because of the joy he's bringing back to the hobby.

Ken Griffey Jr. loves the M1NT case. According to his manager, Griffey takes it with him everywhere and shows it to people with his 1989 Upper Deck rookie card inside.

The card inside the case that Griffey shows off? It's Brian's from when he was young, given to Griffey as a gift when he was invited to The Kid's house to hang out and talk cards.

Likely less than 1 percent of people reading this book know and care about sports cards. If that's you, we just had a connection. If not, using a specific example to make a point is still more effective than speaking in generalities.

Watching Brian's videos made me smile. I messaged him to say thanks.

We spoke on the phone soon after. He told me about M1NT—it hadn't been publicly announced—and said that he was about to look for five investors. I told him not to bother, that I'd take the entire funding round.

Sharing irrational obsession attracts your people to you—friends, customers, promoters, and even investors.

The Algorithm

On December 4, 2009, Google began using algorithms to personalize our internet by invisibly editing our experience of the internet.[7]

"Your filter bubble," according to the internet activist Eli Pariser, "is your own personal, unique universe of information that you live in online."

In 2010, the former CEO of Google Eric Schmidt said, "It will be very hard for people to watch or consume something that has not in some sense been tailored for them."[8]

When asked why a personalized algorithm is so important, Facebook founder Mark Zuckerberg said, "A squirrel dying in front of your house may be more relevant to your interests right now than people dying in Africa."[9] Callous, but also, sadly, true.

Our filter bubbles are online echo chambers. What you see on the internet and what I see on the internet are different, even if we search for the same thing. And what we see is often *all* that we see.

As a result, an almost infinite amount of special interest groups has been created. Each one has celebrities. Each one has somebody famous in that family.

We place importance on things we see often, even if we're the only one who sees them. Exposure therapy is real.

———

SNASA

Christina and her partner owned three CrossFit gyms and were voted the best in their city. They wanted less stress and more profit, so they shut down two locations and built an online program. It was not going well.

"I have stage fright," she said to me on a consulting call.[10]

"I'm so very, *very* new online. That's why I'm scared to talk right now. I don't know the right thing to say or how to talk to people besides just being their friend," she said.

Christina felt stuck. They had a stellar reputation locally. Online, not so much.

Online, they were just another fitness social media account in a sea of wannabe influencers telling people to squat and lunge and do sit-ups and stuff.

Nobody outside of their community in Poughkeepsie knew who they were. And yes, that's a real place. And yes, I will take a field trip there with you. And yes, we can pose for a picture together in front of the city sign, obviously.

"What's your, like, secret nerdy obsession?" I asked Christina.

"What do you mean?" she said.

"Outside of fitness, is there anything that you do where you're like, man, I am unjustifiably obsessed with this thing?" I asked.

"Oh my God. Astrophysics and cometology!" she said.

"So, okay, I saw the craziest comet last week—"

At this point, she interrupted me. Christina went from being shy with stage fright to excitedly interrupting me in less than a minute.

"It sounds like you saw the SpaceX launch from the Jet Propulsion Laboratory in Pasadena," she replied.

She then told me what direction it was moving and described what rocket launches look like in the night sky.

Christina knows how to help people gain muscle and lose fat. She could give it fancy words and film pretty videos, but at the end of the day, that's what she does. The majority of fitness clients just need to eat a bit better and move a bit more. Fitness is simple. It's not easy. But it's simple.

Saying the same things as everybody else is comfortable. It feels safe. But there are tens of thousands of people saying the same nice-sounding words as you online. The secret isn't some video hack or improvement in production quality; it's leaning into your geeky side—finding your own parade—to discover the quiet space. In this case, that space is literally *outer space*.

Imagine if, instead of promoting a "get toned for summer" program like the other 100,000-plus #fitfluencers, Christina formed the *Space Nerd Athleticism and Sexification Association*.

SNASA.

Once formed, her vision becomes clear, marketing more comfortable, and the world less scary. It might even become . . . fun. Let's play with this SNASA concept.

- Rename exercises with an outer space theme. For example, medicine ball slams become "Big Bangs."
- Join online communities with other space geeks.
- Train cometology micro-influencers for free.
- Pitch space blogs and magazines on custom workouts timed around launches and meteor sightings.
- Theme weight loss plans around Pluto, because the gassy ice dwarf has the lowest gravitational pull.
- Send new members an official Snastronaut badge.

Cometology-obsessed fitness isn't a huge pond. But it's big enough. And if Christina formed SNASA, she'd own it.

—

Can They Pay?

Remember Ben Mudge from the beginning of this chapter? What I didn't tell you is that he was supposed to be dead by the age of thirty-eight. Ben has cystic fibrosis.

Chronic illnesses are not only unfair physically, they're unfair financially. Required medicine can be expensive and treatment limiting for certain careers.

Ben wanted to help his community so he built a cheap membership platform with tools, resources, and workouts for people battling CF. It failed.

Acquiring a cheap customer is often just as hard as acquiring a customer who pays a lot. The only difference is that cheap stuff leaves you with less profit.

There wasn't money to acquire members and make Ben's community the valuable resource it needed to be. He shut it down and focused on the *Warhammer* crowd.

He still has clients who have CF and is a champion in the community, but he realized that the best way to help his people wasn't to try to make money off of them—it was to build a highly profitable business elsewhere and use it to serve them.

Russell Brunson, once again from his book *Expert Secrets*, wrote that, "Sometimes people are WILLING to spend money, but they aren't ABLE; they are broke. Other times people have all the money in the world; they are ABLE, but NOT WILLING to part with a dime."

To demonstrate the difference, Brunson gave the example of two people who failed trying to sell information. The first was in the video game market. Kids who his friend attracted wanted the product, but didn't have money. The second provided business development services to engineers. As Brunson said, these people had money but weren't willing to spend it on coaching.

The Obvious Choice finds the geeky submarket that's both willing and able to spend money.

—

The 1 Percent Uniqueness Factor

The following three-stage framework for finding your way comes from my textbook, *The Fundamentals of Online Training*.[11] It's specific to fitness, but can be applied to any industry.

Stage 1: Break down everything you do into four big markets.

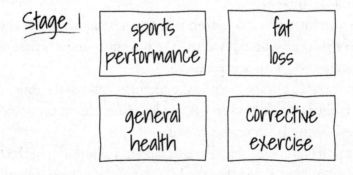

Stage 2: Branch off each market that applies to you into three or four submarkets.

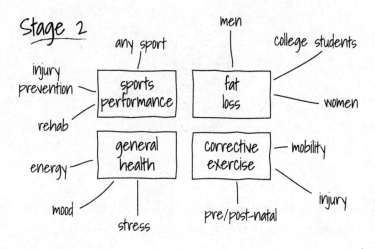

Stage 3: Add in your uniqueness.

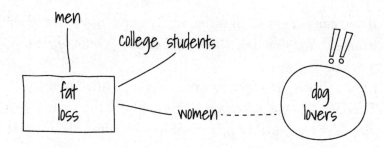

You can download your own 1 percent
Uniqueness worksheet at
www.JonathanGoodman.com/Unique.

Once you've narrowed it down, put your 1 percent Uniqueness Factor through a quick three-part filter:

1. Is it unique?
2. Are people irrationally passionate about it?
3. Are these people both willing and able to spend money?

If you can say yes to all three, you're good to go. Like Rhonda.

Rhonda's the Obvious Choice for humans who want to work out with their dog.

Canine fitness is a serious thing. She's certified in it.

There are special dog-days all throughout the year. There are special days for everything. Literally, everything. They make for great marketing and PR opportunities.

August 8 is National Bowling Day. The first Friday of every November is Love Your Lawyer Day. October 4 is National Taco Day, but tacos are too awesome to have only one day. January 25 is National Fish Taco Day and March 21 is National Crunchy Taco Day.

The special days of the year are easy to build promotions around. All you need is your 1 percent Uniqueness Factor.

For example, January 14 is Dress Up Your Pet Day. Rhonda could reach out to a dog influencer on Instagram and offer to do a collaboration video where she'd buy a costume and they'd film a dog workout.

The month of February is Pet Dental Health Month. She'd team up with doggy dentists for dog workouts.

February 3 is National Golden Retriever Day. She'd collaborate with a popular golden retriever online for a workout.

April 30 is National Adopt a Shelter Pet Day. She'd call up her local news outlets and tell them that she's going to do a human/dog workout to raise money and awareness for the local shelter.[12]

A lot of people in fitness are trying to be the best choice, and are struggling. To her people, Rhonda's the Obvious Choice because she's leaned into the 1 percent that makes her different, not the 99 percent that makes her the same.

Different is better than better.

Next, why smart people tend to make things like getting customers, hiring, and referrals harder than they actually are.

CHAPTER 10

Discover the Easy Answer

Easy Customer Acquisition — Choosing Hard — Easy Hiring — Easy Referrals — Pull the Goalie — The Sesame Street Razor

An interviewer asked Herb Kelleher, the founder and CEO of Southwest Airlines, for his company's trick for getting employees to smile all the time.

"It's easy," said Kelleher. "We just hire smiley people."[1]

Intelligent people tend to overcomplicate things.

———

In low- to middle-income countries, 99 percent of neonatal deaths occur where an infant incubator is cost prohibitive at $25,000. In 2007, graduate students at Stanford were challenged to design one at 1 percent the price.[2]

The team of electrical engineers, computer scientists, and MBA students tested cheaper materials and designed more efficient engineering to bring the costs down. Then they traveled to Kathmandu.

Once in Nepal, they saw empty incubators. The problem, they were told, wasn't a lack of incubators in hospitals. It was that the mothers lived in faraway rural villages with unreliable electricity.

It's not how smart you are, it's how you are smart. Before you try harder, make sure you're on the right path. Before you work on a solution, make sure that you understand the problem.

Babies born prematurely can't regulate their own temperature. Incubators keep their body at 98.6°F.[3] Travel to regional hospitals takes as long as a day (if the mother can afford it). Babies often die en route.

Hospitals didn't need cheaper incubators. Remote medical clinics needed a way to keep babies warm without electricity.

The result was the Embrace Infant Warmer—a portable sleeping bag with a pouch that can be reheated hundreds of times with hot water. It cost $20 to make (a thousand times cheaper than an incubator) and has saved hundreds of thousands of lives.[4]

Perspective is everything.

Spreadsheet-driven ideas are often a misguided default. Blunt force—doing more of the same thing that isn't working, just better or harder or faster—results from insular thinking. Injecting our existing biases shields us from elegant truths.

Complex problems rarely require complex solutions. A few more examples:

The Toronto Transit Commission (TTC) installed a countdown clock at each station. Instead of making trains go faster, they reduced the uncertainty around the wait.

Jay Sorensen invented the coffee cup sleeve in 1991.[5] Instead of designing a more insulated takeaway coffee cup, he made a cheap cover.

Speaking of coffee, Starbucks knows that people are willing to wait longer once they order. Instead of speeding up the drink-making process, they take your order quickly. Easy.

In 2022, the pharmaceutical, vitamin, and supplement industries were worth $660 billion.

The entire rest of the health, fitness, and gym industries combined only generated $30 billion.

That's insane. Cures and quick fixes should not account for twenty-one times more revenue than prevention.[6] Avoiding sickness is obviously more valuable than treating symptoms.

The above stat is appalling for two reasons that don't get talked about enough:

1. Individual intellectual stimulation
2. Prestige

Prevention can't be measured in the moment. The result's an awkward void. In response, we add needless complexity to give us the comforting impression of control.

"Persuading somebody to quit smoking is a psychological exercise. It has nothing to do with molecules and genes and cells. And so, people like me are essentially uninterested in it," said Robert Weinberg, a cancer researcher at MIT. Healing is simply more intellectually stimulating than prevention.[7]

"If there is not the war, you don't get the great general," said Theodore Roosevelt.[8] When something bad happens and it gets fixed, there's a reward. When nothing bad happens, there's nothing to fix, and nobody gets rewarded. That's a mind-boggling concept to wrap my mind around.

To be clear, cancer researchers like Robert Weinberg do important work. Treatment is enormously valuable. But it's fascinating to consider how much both individual intellectual stimulation and prestige impact our approach to solving our own problems.

From a young age, we've been indoctrinated to think that it has to be hard if it's going to work. That's simply not true.

My goal with this chapter is to show you an easier way to get customers, hire, and generate referrals in a few thousand short words. A tall task.

But first, a quick story about how slow people were to use seat belts.

——

Easy Customer Acquisition

In 1955, 37,000 Americans died in car accidents. Adjust that for miles driven and it's six times today's rate, or 258,000 deaths.

That same year, Ford began offering seat belts in cars for $27 ($300 in 2023, adjusted for inflation). Despite research showing a 70 percent reduced fatality rate, only 2 percent of customers upgraded to seat belts in 1956.

Congress mandated that all cars be outfitted with seat belts in 1968. Using them was voluntary. Most Americans didn't. As late as 1983, seat belt usage was *still* less than 15 percent. It took almost fifty years for seat belt usage to increase to more than 80 percent.[9]

Most humans never change. They like what they like, and they do what they do. In some cases, like with seat belts, change eventually comes but it's agonizingly slow.

Resisting change is completely normal human behavior.

And so, if you need people to change in order to buy your thing, you're playing the game of business on hard mode. It's far easier to find people already doing the thing you want them to do and get them to do more of it.

These days, Joel Weldon's a Hall of Fame professional speaker. He struggled early on though. In 1971, it took him 1,200 calls to make one sale of Earl Nightingale success tapes.

"It was $175 for six cassettes and a loose-leaf book [about $1,300 in 2023, adjusted for inflation]. And we had to provide a tape recorder because people didn't even have a cassette recorder in those days. . . . I was calling on people that I knew could benefit from this. And they would listen to it, but they couldn't afford it or didn't want to spend the money," said Weldon.

In desperation, Weldon called the most successful person he knew: a real estate developer named David Jones. Within five minutes of David hearing a Nightingale tape, he said: "Stop. There's more of these? I want them."

"You want them? You're the most successful guy that I know. Why would you want this?" Weldon asked.

"Because I need to be reminded," said David.

Joel admitted his troubles, telling David that he was calling people who needed help—those struggling in their marriage and business—but nobody was buying.

"You're talking to the wrong people. You've gotta talk to successful people," said David.

Weldon learned his lesson and made the change. In the years that followed, he became the top salesperson in the Nightingale-Conant organization.

"When you're selling success, you call on successful people. When you're selling improvement, you call on people already committed to improvement. If you look in the gym, who are the people already in the gym? Fit people!" said Weldon.[10]

People who buy, buy lots. People who don't, don't.

A few examples:

- **If you sell silicon baby toys**, team up with home air purification system companies. Parents who care about removing toxins, care lots.
- **If you write fan fiction**, focus on existing readers. People who read, read lots.

- **If you make fancy cheese**, produce weekly reviews of the best crackers. People who snack, snack lots. (Ask me how I know.)

Trying to convince somebody to change in order to buy from you is hard. Instead, find people already doing the thing you help people do and get them to do more of it with you.

Today, Clay Hebert is one of the most sought-after brand strategists in the United States. When he was young, he sold chocolate bars in front of a grocery store as part of a school fundraiser.

Clay's key insight was that, "It's not about the candy bar. It's about the person wanting to support a kid bundled up freezing his toes off because he had to stand outside."

"And so," Clay said, "I did my first, and hopefully last (slightly), unethical marketing strategy, which was, I brought my older brother's clothes in a grocery bag and when about six of the people had bought the candy bars on the way in, I ran around the corner, changed my clothes, and those same people bought on the way out."[11]

James is a guy I know who sells online coaching packages for $5,000 while many of his colleagues struggle to charge $50.

If I told you his real name, you wouldn't be able to find him online. He doesn't use social media, run ads, or have a website. His entire web presence is an application form hosted on Google.

It wasn't always this way. Not long ago, David was struggling. His paid ads weren't converting.

As a last resort, he invested everything he had into a business mastermind. It cost $10,000. He spread the investment out over twelve months. His initial goal was to learn how to write better advertising copy, create more compelling content, and run more effective paid ads. He thought those were the only ways to get clients.

Mindset, mental health, fitness, and nutrition questions always came up in the mastermind's private community. David gave detailed answers. He became the de facto wellness expert in this group of high achievers.

The mastermind was full of men who are already investing $10,000-plus a year on personal development. This means:

1. These men have money.
2. These men spend money.
3. These men are already investing in coaching for themselves to build a better future.

People who hire expensive online coaches, hire a lot of coaches. And people who don't, don't.

Members of the mastermind began hiring him.

Realizing that he had stumbled upon a gold mine, David joined another mastermind with the income from his first three clients and repeated the process. He now spends upward of $100,000 a year on these groups and makes more than a million dollars. David hasn't created a piece of content on social media or paid for an advertisement since.

If a costly mastermind doesn't exist, the example doesn't apply to you, or it's simply too expensive for you to join right now, then make your own group, community, or event.

For example, if I owned a flower shop and wanted to become the Obvious Choice, I'd start a group of local growers to share tips and tricks.

Then I'd create a series of categoric awards for best local gardens and host a yearly garden gala (sponsored by other local businesses) where people dress up and drink bubbly alcoholic drinks from silly thin glasses while we announce the winners.

I'd then print yard signs for the participants to proudly display on their lawns announcing their nominations and awards with my flower shop's name placed prominently, of course.

Why? Because people who garden buy flowers. And people who don't, don't.

—

Choosing Hard

Easy doesn't necessarily mean better. You might choose hard.

Real quick, let me explain.

There's a joke in the fitness industry that fit people don't belong in the gym. "You're done, go home." But that's not how it goes, of course. Already fit people invest the most time and money on fitness, despite needing it least.

The easiest way to make money in fitness is to target already fit people and ignore anybody out of shape.

Caring people say they want to help people. The sad reality is that some people aren't willing to invest in being helped.

I wish it weren't this way.

There's different definitions of professional success. If you work in fitness, you may decide that, even though it'll be harder to build a business, it's personally more rewarding to help inactive or over-weight people.

There's no right or wrong. There is, however, easier and harder.

You might still decide to tackle harder problems for reasons that can be quite noble. Many do.

—

Easy Hiring

Four Seasons Hotels and Resorts employs 45,000 people. Their recruitment and hiring are robust.

To hire his first-ever employee, though, Isadore "Issy" Sharp, the founder of the Four Seasons, didn't accept résumés. Instead, he walked into the most popular hotel in Toronto at the time (the Westbury) and asked the manager if he knew anybody looking for a job. The manager introduced him to Ian Munro.

According to Issy in the podcast *Big Shot*, here's how the interview went:

> I went in and met this man. I talked to him about what I was intending to do and he gave me his list of things he had done. And we had a nice, charming conversation.
>
> So, I hired him.
>
> Now, I don't know how to interview people and how to hire people. I'm a twenty-five-year-old construction guy. And, well, that became the beginning.[12]

Issy knew what he didn't know.

"Hire slow, fire fast," they say. And maybe that's good advice. But in my experience, people make it harder than it needs to be early on.

All the advice I've seen about hiring is for large companies, ignoring the fact that all large companies started as small companies. And when those smaller companies hired early on, they didn't know what they were doing.

Interviewing somebody for a job is almost impossibly difficult. Professionals who dedicate their lives to it only make the right choice 30 percent of the time.

———

An Instagram page that I follow with 650,000 followers put a post up looking for their first staff member—a half-time customer service rep. The next day, they posted a story saying that they got five hundred responses and were reading each one and asking their audience to "please be patient."

What an incredible waste of time.

They have an app. It would have taken them twenty minutes to scan community posts and find a naturally helpful and empathetic person, reach out, and offer the job.

When you're looking to hire early on, admit your ignorance. Like Issy, start by finding people already doing the thing.

Think, where's the skill you need already being demonstrated at a high level?

I had lunch with the guy who ran the USA department of one of the biggest blender companies. He told me about his first day on the job with the company's president. (The following conversation's paraphrased.)

"Don't sit down. We're going recruiting," the president said.

They walked into a toy store in New York City. Supposedly, this store hired theater performers and dressed them up as movie characters.

Our company, the president explained, sells through live demonstrations in stores like Costco. "Teaching our staff about blenders is the easy part. What we need are performers who can engage a crowd," the president said.

The toy store did the hard work of finding improv actors and putting them on display. The president walked up to the best ones and handed them a card saying, "If you ever want to make real money, give me a call." Recruiting, done.

One more example.

For eight years, I published a weekly roundup of the best fitness content on the internet. It became the industry standard. Tens of thousands of personal trainers relied on us to curate their ongoing education.

I needed to hire two people from outside my company to choose its contents. On a Friday night at 7:45 p.m., I posted a note on Facebook that said: "If you're reading fitness blogs right now, send me a message with the last two posts you read. I want to pay you for what you're doing."

Only obsessive nerds read fitness blogs on Friday nights. It was an easy job search. Took fifteen minutes.

———

Easy Referrals

Today, Giovanni "Gio" Marsico runs the Archangel Academy, one of the largest communities of heart-centered entrepreneurs. In 2006, he was a marketing consultant that turned a little fitness studio into a multimillion-dollar business.

First, Gio wrote a list of all the other places where a member at the gym might also invest time, energy, and money. Next, he surveyed the gym members, asking for their favorites out of his list that included tanning salons, hairdressers, massage therapy clinics, spas, chiropractors, and more.

Think, who are *your* people and what other businesses like yours do they buy from?

With the data from the survey, he called the top choices from each category. Here's an example of what he said:

"Hey, I'm from Bodies by Design. We asked our members what their favorite spa in the area was and you were number one. Can we send more people to you?"

Of course they said yes.

He then asked for an introductory offer or discount to pass along and included it in a booklet of gift certificates distributed to the gym members called *Our Favorite Places*.

This step ingratiated him to the other businesses.

Giovanni then wrote a letter for each of the other businesses to send out to their customers that said, "We already know a lot of you love Bodies by Design. If you're not already a member, Chris, the owner, wants to pay for your first session. Here's three $90 gift certificates for you and two of your friends."

Overnight, and with very little effort, Bodies by Design became the Obvious Choice in their community.[13]

There's three rules to follow when getting referrals from other businesses:

1. Give before getting.
2. Make it easy for the other business owner.
3. Make it compelling for the customer.

Whenever somebody asks me what to do because their content isn't converting, I know that they're hoping for an algorithm hack or conversion secret, as though there's something almost mystically complicated that they're missing and that, once they figure it out, all their problems will be solved.

Instead, I ask them to tell me about the best customer they've ever worked with. After they answer, I'll ask where the customer came from.

I've gone through this process at least thirty times. They've never answered "social media." Not once. It's always been some kind of a word-of-mouth referral. And yet, they still focus on social media, posting multiple times a week, chocking up referrals to luck, chance, or happenstance.

I want to be clear: social media *can* work. It's just hard. Ignoring the work to create the content, people on social media have no reason to trust you. To them, you're just another person on the internet.

The easiest sale you'll ever make is to a referred customer.

Referrals can come from complementary businesses like the previous example. Or they can come from existing customers. But, as you'll learn in the next example from an online company, asking for referrals from existing customers doesn't work. Making your customer feel like an all-star, on the other hand, does.

Mike Doehla ran an online nutrition coaching company called StrongerU. He'd give his successful clients gift cards to their favorite stores for new clothing because their old stuff didn't fit. It wasn't a gift card for a referral. It was a way for them to celebrate their own success.

Buying new clothing after losing weight is a big deal. His clients rightfully celebrated it (with Mike's encouragement) by taking pictures at the store and posting them to social media.

Their friends and family would congratulate them and send messages asking how they lost the weight. Mike got referred.[14]

After doing this for a few years, Mike sold his coaching company for eight figures and retired in his thirties.[15]

Referrals are hard to teach because they're a psychological lesson, not an economic one. In terms of monetary value, it's always a bad deal for customers. They're sending you a valuable customer and in exchange you're giving them, what . . . a gift card to a coffee shop?

It's a social trade, not an economic one. Make your customers feel like the all-star that they are, and they'll send you more business than you know what to do with.

Referrals can also come from the local community. One final example:

My son finished a week of summer camp. He won the "community" award for his group.

Don't be impressed. Every kid wins an award every week.

The next day, I noticed a sign on our lawn that said, "My son just won the community award at Super Fun Time Sports Camp" (name changed for privacy reasons). The camp put it there.

Brilliant.

My son was proud of the award. We left the sign up for a while. Our neighbor saw it and asked if my son liked the camp. I said yes. They registered their kid for the following week.

You can access a fabulous podcast episode that goes deeper into referrals with additional examples and more nuanced techniques at www.JonathanGoodman.com/Referral.

Pull the Goalie

If a hockey team is losing at the end of the game, the coach removes the goalie in favor of an extra attacker.

It's a risk that gives the losing team a better chance at scoring a goal to tie the game but also increases their chance of getting scored on and being embarrassed.

Convention is to pull the goalie with one or two minutes left. Every red-blooded Canadian knows that. Data, however, suggests a different story.

According to *Pulling the Goalie: Hockey and Investment Opportunities*, it's irresponsible to wait that long. Instead, a goalie should be pulled with:

- 6:10 left in the game when down by one goal.
- 11:30 left in the game when down by two goals.

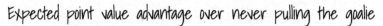

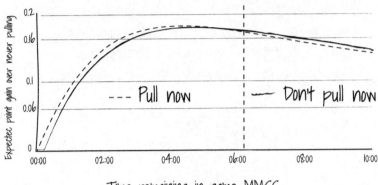

Expected point value advantage over never pulling the goalie

Asness, Cliff S., and Brown, Aaron, "Pulling the Goalie: Hockey and Investment Implications," March 1, 2018. Available at SSRN: https://ssrn.com/abstract=3132563.

Sorry. Not sure what I'm sorry about. But the Canadian in me feels like saying sorry.

Pulling your goalie nearly quadruples the probability of your opponent scoring, while not even doubling your own chance of scoring.[16]

Standing points matter; goals don't. Losing by two goals (or ten) is no worse than losing by one. Both result in zero standing points. Therefore, a team gains a lot by scoring, and loses little by getting scored on.

Practicing optimal goalie pulling gains an average of 0.05 more points per game. In an eighty-two-game season, that's an extra 4.18 points—enough to make a material difference in the end-of-year standings. So what if the losses were blowouts?

Entrenched conventions are often wrong.

Data plays a central role in other major sports. It's led to more three-point attempts in basketball, shorter starts by pitchers in baseball, and risky fourth-down conversion attempts in football like the one by the Philadelphia Eagles in the 2018

Super Bowl where quarterback Nick Foles caught a pass in the end zone.[17]

Going for it at fourth and goal down three points in the second quarter was a risky play call by Doug Pederson, the coach of the Eagles. Convention was to kick the easy field goal to tie the game. If the trick play didn't work, it would have gone down as one of the worst play calls in history. Pederson was going to be the hero or the loser.

Coaches aren't actually rewarded for winning. They're rewarded for being perceived as good coaches. The two are closely related but aren't the same thing.

"Sins of commission are far more obvious than sins of omission. The hockey coach who pulls his goalie down 0–2 with ten minutes to go and loses 0–5 will face harsh criticism from every quarter. A coach who quietly loses 1–2, pulling his goalie only in the final minute, can hold his head up and say his guys played hard but the puck didn't roll their way tonight; it was a close game, and they'll work even harder to get the breaks tomorrow," wrote Clifford Asness and Aaron Brown, the authors of the paper on pulling the goalie.

"Essentially, winning ugly is undervalued versus losing elegantly; and losing ugly can be career suicide," they added.

We humans have competing motivations:

1. To make the right decision, and
2. To feel like we can justify why we made a decision if things go wrong.

Following misguided conventions and losing preserves our status. Disagreeability, even when you're objectively correct, feels risky.

"We become good at what we practice even if what we are practicing is not good for us," wrote Dandapani, a Hindu priest and entrepreneur coach. "Where awareness goes, energy flows," he added.

"The best way to understand this statement," said Dandapani, "is to look at energy the same way you look at water. If I took a watering can and I watered a garden bed, would the weeds or the flowers grow? The answer is both, because water has no ability to differentiate between weeds and flowers. Whatever gets watered in the garden will start to grow. Energy works in exactly the same way."[18]

Discovering your easy is really about focusing your energy on the right problems, even if it challenges the way things are "supposed" to be done.

Pull the goalie.

———

The *Sesame Street* Razor

Shane Snow's a science and business journalist who gets hired to force executives to watch *Sesame Street*.[19]

In one episode, Elmo wants to give a cookie to his friend, a rock. The rock doesn't have a mouth. Uh, cause it's a rock. . .

Snow then asks the executives how Elmo's feeling. They say that Elmo's mad and that the rock is delusional because it doesn't have a mouth.

"That's technically incorrect," said Snow.

"We can't observe that Elmo is mad because we can't feel his feelings. What we observe is that he raised his voice. What we observe is that he's throwing his hands up in the air. What we observe is that the color of his face changed. Based on that, one of our hypotheses is that he's mad, but that leaves room for Elmo to tell us that he's not mad; he's frustrated."

Smart people think too fast, assume patterns too readily, and jump to conclusions too quickly. It closes us off to opportunities. Snow suggests that we slow down. That we observe, not react.

The beginning of this chapter told the story of the Embrace Infant Warmer. The team from Stanford was tasked with making a cheaper baby incubator. This constraint led to experiments with materials and engineering.

The problem, however, wasn't that lower-income countries needed cheaper baby incubators—it was that they needed to keep neonatal babies alive.

When they reframed the question—"How the heck does an incubator keep a baby alive?"—they discovered that regulating body heat was the key ingredient. A single insight resulting from a better question saved hundreds of thousands of lives.

A friend asked me how to make more engaging Instagram content to attract customers.

But my friend doesn't want Instagram growth; she wants more customers. By assuming that IG's the way to go, she's shutting herself off from all other ways to get customers.

Smart people wrongly inject assumed answers into questions.

The *Sesame Street* Razor states that you must never disguise your hypothesis as the question.

The corollary to the razor is that our brains solve problems better by working backward than they do forward. A trick is to assume that the problem has already been solved and retrace the steps.

I asked my friend to tell me the name of the best customer she'd ever worked with. Then I asked her where that customer came from.

It was a referral. Her business was 90 percent referrals. Instagram has never generated her a good customer.

We then began the process of tracing back the last ten referrals, mapping the sources, and building a plan for scaled outreach in similar places.

Instead of creating content for IG, she took the best material she's already produced, branded it for collaborative partners, and allowed them to distribute it locally in their clinics and through their mailing lists along with a gift card for her service as a value add. Less work, better results.

Easy feels like cheating. Hard feels like progress.

When things feel harder than they should, pause. Ask yourself: What problem am I solving and is there an easier way?

Want better customers? Find people already buying a service similar to yours.

Want to hire? Work backward from the primary attribute you need. Go to where it's already on display.

Want referrals? Design a way for others to feel like they look good by talking about you.

There's a saying that if you want to achieve a great time for swimming 100 meters, it's a lot easier to swim with the tide than it is to work on your stroke.

Stop making it harder than it already is.

Next, it's time to become famous to the family.

CHAPTER 11

Become Famous to the Family

Sapphire and the Mayor — The Best of Etobicoke (TBE) — *Four Coffees*

S eth Godin wrote: "You need to be famous to the small circle of people you are hoping will admire and trust you. . . . Being famous to the family is far more efficient than being famous to everyone."

Trust needs touch. Large audiences are inefficient for deepening relationships.

Godin later added, "It takes focus, though."

He's right. That's the hard part.

There's so much pressure these days to impress people we don't know, don't care about, and won't ever do business with that it's easy to forget about all the people we do care about and can actually do business with.

Let's develop a marketing system together.

Despite all the incredible advances in technology, the best marketing to humans by humans can be summed up in three words: talk to people.

Which people? Your people.

What do you say? Not much; you mostly listen.

Where do you find them? Wherever they already are.

Developing a Human Optimized Marketing System (HOMS) requires answering five key questions:

1. What key benefit does my thing provide?
2. Who are my customers?
3. What do they want?
4. Where am I going to find them?
5. How can I talk to them today?

All of this fits on a sticky note.

Sapphire and the Mayor

Rahul Gopal believes every child has the ability to learn.[1]

Tutoring is mostly a side-hustle industry. There's no regulation or designation. As a result, some tutors, like Rahul, are serious and the majority aren't.

Once people hire his company, assuming they've hired tutors in the past, they'll notice the difference. But that only happens *after* he gets hired.

Canvassing schools, paid ads, and buying booths at street festivals every weekend are common marketing methods. They work fine, but there's a better way.

Rahul's Human Optimized Marketing System (HOMS):

1. *What key benefit does his product or service provide?* Customized educational support.
2. *Who are his customers?* Wealthy parents.
3. *What do they want?* Individualized attention and a better future for their child.
4. *Where is he going to find them?* At charity galas.
5. *How can he talk to them today?* By buying a ticket and attending.

Wealthy people have kids who they desperately want to see excel in school. For the affluent, money isn't a concern; time is.

Charity galas are rare events where the affluent are accessible. Rahul's the only tutor investing his marketing budget on attending them.

All it takes is a quick handshake and a "what do you do for work?" chat for Rahul to say that he "helps kids build confidence through learning when they're young and prepares high school kids to get into the best colleges." Phone numbers are exchanged, referrals are made.

When you work backward and get yourself in the right rooms, good things reliably happen.

There's luck involved. Not every event works. But affluent communities are well-connected. Once you're in, you're in.

Have you ever wondered how things like large-scale, government-sponsored tutoring contracts get handed out?

There isn't exactly a number you can call and say, "Hi, um, I'd like to speak to the government. Hi, yes. Good to meet you, Mrs. G. I tutor kids and think you should create an inner-city program that doesn't exist yet. You will? Great. I would like the contract."

Rahul met the mayor of Toronto one night at a charity function that cost $2,500 a plate. The mayor needed a tutor for his niece and trusted him because of their shared connection to the charity. Unbeknownst to Rahul, an inner-city tutoring project was about to be funded, and he was asked to bid on the contract.

The price of admission—$2,500—might seem like a lot to spend on one evening. But compare the impact of spending it this way with paid advertisements to cold traffic that's going to require a well-oiled sales process, hours, and money, creating content, or paying for booths at street festivals, spending every weekend in the summer begging passersby to talk.

In every case, it must feel random when Rahul gets referred.

Somebody he'd be seated at a table with for a fundraiser *just happened* to have had dinner with their rich CEO friend the week before who was complaining that their kid was struggling in school. But that's how this stuff happens. That's how this stuff *always* happens.

Rahul doesn't appear on TV whenever local news outlets need an education expert. And he's definitely not famous on the internet. Instead, he's famous to the family—the Obvious Choice for education support among affluent parents in Toronto.

Next, exactly what I'd do if I were starting a new business today.

___

The Best of Etobicoke (TBE)

The French philosopher Jean de La Bryuère once said, "The shortest and best way of making your fortune is to let people clearly see that it is in their interests to promote yours."[2]

I live in a pocket of Toronto called Etobicoke. Recommendations, not flyers, help me discover everything from coffee shops to massage therapists to chiropractors and even, admittedly only from my one excessively spiritual friend down the street, upstairs strip mall fortune tellers.

If I were starting a new business in the area, I'd launch a podcast called *The Best of Etobicoke*.

Being a podcaster and using a podcast to become the Obvious Choice are two different games you get to choose from. We conventionally think of podcasts as ways to broadcast ourselves to the world. They're much better tools to make us family to the family.

You'd get ignored (or blocked by a secretary) 9.9 times out of 10 if you were to call the CEO of the biggest businesses in your community inquiring whether they were interested in hearing more about what you do.

You'd reverse those odds by asking if they were interested in appearing on your podcast, *The Best of Etobicoke,* which shares stories and wisdom from the leaders in your community.

In *How to Win Friends and Influence People*, Dale Carnegie wrote, "The deepest urge in human nature is 'the desire to be important.'"[3] The secret to getting what you want in life is to give others what they want.

Everyone wants improved status.

I love talking about me. You love talking about you. The CEO you're interviewing loves talking about herself, too.

Once done, they'll know you, like you, and trust you. After the episode, if they have any desire for your product or service, they might become a customer and/or refer others.

After each interview, ask your guest for an introduction to two others for your show. Simply by virtue of having a podcast, successful people in your community will be making introductions on your behalf. Said another way: they'll be referring you.

You won't, however, have a lot of listeners. It'll play on your mind.

Your show will never hit the "best of" podcast charts. You'll never be able to brag about how many downloads you have.

What you will have done is hacked your way into a stellar network of wealthy and well-connected people who want to see you succeed. As a bonus, you didn't have to dance like a monkey on the internet to do it.

Two real-world examples:

Greg Finch is a mental and physical performance coach for surfers. He uses the *Surf Strong* podcast to become famous to the international surf family.

Greg's Human Optimized Marketing System:

1. *What key benefit does his product or service provide?* Mental and physical performance improvements.
2. *Who are his customers?* Wealthy surfers.
3. *What do they want?* Better mental performance at work and better strength and stamina while surfing.
4. *Where is he going to find them?* At expensive surf resorts, charitable surf foundations, tech companies that service the surf industry, and so on.
5. *How can he talk to them today?* By starting a podcast as a networking tool.

Without recording a single episode, simply because he called it a podcast and had an image he mocked up on a free design app, Greg booked his first eight interviews.

His initial guests included:

- The medical director for the World Surf League
- The community outreach director for the Mauli Ola Foundation (a charity promoting surfing as an alternate therapy for genetic disorders)
- An executive coach who loves surfing

- A physiotherapist who treats surfers on the island of Kauai in Hawaii

Anytime somebody he's interviewed for his show encounters a person who wants either mindset or physical training, Greg gets referred. He's quietly adding one to two premium clients each week, paying $1,500 each. It feels random every time. But it's not, of course.

Another example:

Billy Hofacker's a financial consultant for fitness professionals. He uses the *Your Fitness Money Coach* podcast to become famous to the personal trainer and gym owner family.

In the past week he's published two episodes, spoken at his industry's biggest online industry event with a talk titled "Get Rid of Money Stress for Good," and done a live interview in a Facebook group.

Billy's Human Optimized Marketing System:

1. *What key benefit does his product or service provide?* Financial coaching and education.
2. *Who are his customers?* Personal trainers and gym owners in the United States.
3. *What do they want?* More money and a better understanding of money.
4. *Where is he going to find them?* Industry events and communities.
5. *How can he talk to them today?* By interviewing the people who run the events and communities.

A podcast about money specifically for personal trainers can't have more than fifty to a hundred listeners per episode. That's a good thing. **The more exclusive we are, the more inclusive we become.**

"People believe something that only does one thing is better at that thing than something that does that thing and something else," said Rory Sutherland.[4] Who told me via email that this is often called the "Jack-of-All-Trades" heuristic.

Billy's decision to focus on a tiny market cut him off from approximately 99.7 percent of possible clients and made him the Obvious Choice for the remaining 0.3 percent.

On one hand, doing unscalable things cuts you off from potential opportunities. On the other hand, it's a useful constraint. There's no wasted effort, no comparison, no praying to the social media gods, and no burnout. It's precision. Focus.

By not trying to become famous on the internet, Billy's become famous to the family.

—

Promoting the show is your responsibility.

Here's how I'd growth-hack *The Best of Etobicoke*:

TBE would feature two types of interviews: One would feature the business leaders. The other would tell the stories of all the little local establishments that make my community so wonderful.

I love my home. And yet, I feel no connection to the people who serve our community. I can't help but think I'm not alone.

For example, I write in a simultaneously misplaced and perfectly placed Turkish coffee shop. It's called the Galata Cafe and is owned by Caglar Araz—an immigrant who wanted to bring his country's culture to Canada.[5]

I want to know Caglar's story. How did he end up there? Why did he build such a wonderful cafe?

I'd title the episode, "How the Heck Did Such a Wonderful Turkish Cafe End Up in Etobicoke (of All Places)?" Once it's live, I'd print hundreds of cards with Caglar's face and the title of the episode.

The cards would have a QR code that leads people to a page on my website with a link to listen to the episode. This would be the same website as my company, and each podcast episode card would also include my company name. There's a badly drawn example coming up.

I'd drop off these cards at the Galata Cafe and say to Caglar: "Hearing your story made this cafe even more special to me. It makes me want to come back. I think it will do the same for others who listen, so I made these cards to make it easy for you to recommend that your patrons listen to your interview. Can I leave them with you to have your staff hand one out to everybody who orders?"

Picture this: It's Sunday morning and you're going for a stroll with the family. On your right in a nondescript strip mall you notice a sign that says "Galata—Turkish Cafe." You look at your wife and point. She shrugs her shoulders.

Once inside, you're transported to Turkey.

It doesn't look or smell like a ratty strip mall in Etobicoke anymore.

You decide what you want and laugh at yourself trying to say the names on the Turkish menu, grab a little flag with your order number, and sit down.

The food comes. It's fresh and flavorful. Then Caglar walks out with Turkish coffee in a tiny cup sitting on the bottom of a gilded birdcage. Beside the cup is a single square of Turkish delight.

You and your wife have stumbled on something special. You've been transported to another place—a place where details matter and every sip and bite are more delicious than the last. Then you look out the window and remember that you're in a quiet strip mall in Etobicoke and you think, *How the heck did this place end up here?*

As if Caglar has read your mind, his staff brings you your check with this card stapled to it:

I'd scan the QR code to download and listen to the episode. Because of my personal connection to the space and proximity of it to my home, it'd bypass everything else.

How the Heck Did a Wonderful
Turkish Cafe End up in Etobicoke?

Listen to Caglar's
amazing story

The Best of Etobicoke podcast is presented by
Jonathan Goodman's Fabulous and Fantabulous Coaching
for People Who Want Strong Bodies and Stuff.

Never forget that when you enter a small business, you're entering a manifestation of the owner's dream. It's special, and so are they. Small business ownership is hard. Support them. Celebrate them. Community businesses aren't zero-sum games. Together, you rise. Together, you win. The best way to get yours is to help others get theirs.

—

Build once, market twice.

The best marketing includes leverage, positive-sum games, and transference of trust.

Every few weeks I'd pop back into Galata with more cards to hand out (and eat a sandwich, of course).

I'd follow this process with the top coffee shops, restaurants, physiotherapists, and, of course, purveyors of fine foreign cheeses in my community. If each shop has fifty to a hundred customers a day, my business would get promoted hundreds of times a week through local recommendations.

Through *The Best of Etobicoke* podcast, I'd be friends with the most important people in my community and would have dozens of local businesses sharing my business within four to six months. The world at large wouldn't know about me, but I'd be famous in my local community.

After typing this section, I didn't want to publish it because it's so cool. A part of me wants to keep it to myself. I love this idea almost as much as I love Turkish sandwiches. Almost.

—

Four Coffees

"There's a cafe owner in one of our buildings that built her entire business by taking four cups of coffee to each of the neighboring businesses every day," says Chris Cooper, the owner of Two-Brain Business Consulting.[6]

Why doesn't every cafe do this?

You don't need to own a cafe to bring people coffee. Cooper says every local business owner should buy four coffees every morning and bring them to a neighboring shop.

Dr. Robert Cialdini's first principle of persuasion in his book *Influence* states that human beings are wired to return favors. Reciprocity compels us to give back more value than we received in the first place.

What stops people from doing this is not buying the coffee. It costs $10. What stops them is the worry of what to say next.

"The goal," Cooper said, "is to take them coffee. Not to sell them anything."

I love that. There's clarity and simplicity in obviousness.

Becoming famous to the family is as simple as talking to people, offering them value, and not expecting anything in return.

What are the best shops to go into? I don't know.

What's the max radius around your place to network in? Not sure.

How often should you go back to the same shop? I don't know that either.

This isn't an exact science. In business, the best strategies never are. And that's why most people don't do them.

Maybe turn it into a ritual. Choose four businesses for each day of the week. Every Monday show up to four, Tuesday a different four, and so on. Begin with the places closest to you and work your way outward.

Or, do it a different way.

Four coffees can be literal or metaphorical. It means a gift—something easy, cost-effective, repeatable, and meaningful—given to a member of the family you want to become famous to.

Luka Hocevar[7] generates hundreds of leads every month with a Saturday morning charity fitness boot camp. The entire community is involved. Local businesses both donate and participate.

He built his network by walking into neighboring stores, asking for the owner by name, and saying: "Hey, I'm Luka. I own the gym down the street. I want us all to win together. If you have a few minutes, I'd love to tell you about a few things that are working well for us building our business."

Not sure what to say?

Give them a gift of a book that helped you. Maybe it's this one. Buy a few dozen copies of this book and tag some pages with sticky notes. Hand them out to neighboring businesses. Talk about why you found a particular insight useful.

———

It's 4:45 a.m. on January 9, 2024. Most of this book was written before sunrise. During the day, I run two businesses, exercise, and try to be the best dad to my two young boys.

This book's release date is a year away. That means that I have a year to market it. But, I'm busy. Not only that, I'm in San Juan del Sur, Nicaragua. Giving physical gifts isn't an option.

On a Google doc I wrote, "Take the next year to systematically expand my network in three or four key markets." What markets? To narrow it down, I asked myself three questions:

1.   Who can my book help?
2.   What do I know and embody?
3.   What people already share publicly?

This book can help a lot of people. I had to narrow it down for promotional purposes. I started with who I am, which is an author who has a background in fitness and packs his stuff into a backpack to live abroad three to five months a year.

Next, I know that people who share, share lots. And people who don't, don't.

My goal is to generate word of mouth.

With that in mind, targeting communities that already talk about what they love makes sense.

I settled on the following four markets:

1. Writer / indie author / self-publishing
2. Personal training
3. CrossFit
4. Minimalist / digital nomad

Next up, my Four Coffee plan, which I call, "catch people in the act of doing something good and become their biggest fan."

The two principles are:

1. Default to generosity.
2. Never resist a kind impulse.

I don't have much spare time. Fortunately, consistency trumps intensity. Small actions chosen strategically and executed systematically add up.

Jen Gottlieb, a motivational speaker, once shared that she does all her networking in fifteen minutes a day.[8] "I go into my Instagram and I have a spreadsheet of people that I want to build relationships with. I engage with their content so they start seeing me every day. Then when I meet them, I've already provided the value and they're like, 'Oh man, how can I help you? Thank you so much for commenting and buying my book and sharing about it.'"

First, I've built a list of fifty to a hundred people in each market, with the top priority being podcasters who host interview shows. I've subscribed to their email newsletters and social media platforms.

Every day I choose ten to fifteen from the list and open recent content that they've produced. I do some combination of commenting, replying, and sharing it. If they're coming out with a product or service, I'll buy it and publicly share when I do. If they announce an upcoming project like their own book launch, I'll save the date and set a reminder to order and review it right away.

People don't need to live physically close to you. Choose your family, and then support them.

For the next year, this is how I'm marketing my book. It takes thirty minutes a day.

Four Coffees.

—

Okay, fine. I'll admit it: HOMS is a terrible acronym.

If nobody's around you, say it out loud. It'll sound like you're in a meditation circle run by some dude from Southern California who's wearing a feather necklace and chanting while playing a Himalayan sound bowl before he practices breathwork in a bucket of ice.

The acronym is weird because it has the word "human" in it.

Making an acronym with an "h" is surprisingly difficult.

But you sell stuff to humans, and marketing these days feels so (in)human. It shouldn't be that way. And I hope you now feel empowered knowing that it doesn't have to be.

Now let me tell you how Google decides to spend a large part of its $3 billion innovation budget. It involves monkeys.

CHAPTER 12

#MonkeyFirst

*Pirates of the World — $846,706 — Getting
Jiggy — Permission to Launch*

A lot more people fail because they don't have enough sales than go under from lack of a logo.

Beware of false progress.

—

Google invests more than $3 billion a year into an innovations lab called X. It's devoted to solving impossible problems and guided by a philosophy called "Monkeys and Pedestals."[1]

Dr. Eric "Astro" Teller, because of course that's his nickname, the leader of X, uses the example of trying to get a monkey to recite Shakespeare. That's not a funny enough mental image for me. I'm going to change it to a monkey juggling flaming sticks.

Imagine that you're trying to teach a monkey to juggle fire as part of a performance. There are two jobs:

1. Teaching a monkey to juggle fire
2. Building the pedestal for it to stand on

Where do you begin?

Many people would start with the pedestal because it feels like progress. It'll cost money and take time, but you know that you can build it. "That's the worst possible choice," said Teller. "You can always build the pedestal. All the risk and learning comes with the extremely hard work of first training the monkey."[2]

A pedestal's useless if the monkey isn't juggling fire. Who wants to watch a monkey aflame onstage because some asshole human made it throw flaming sticks in the air, anyway?

Your business has lots of pedestals but only one monkey.

Pedestal tasks:

- Setting up a legal corporation
- Designing a logo
- Creating content
- Buying the "best" mic, software, and camera
- Building a website
- Configuring a productivity app

Monkey task:

- Selling

The first step must come before the second. A business is nothing more than an unproven idea before it makes its first sale.

Things like forming a legal corporation and getting a logo may be hard, time intensive, and expensive, but you know you can do them. Then there's sales. Does anybody actually want your thing? Will they pay money for it? Because if they don't, none of the other stuff matters. #MonkeyFirst.

In a 2008 talk for the startup accelerator Y Combinator, Jeff Bezos said that "one way to look at the future of something is to find an analog from the past."[3] He then described his experience touring a three-hundred-year-old Belgium brewery.

According to Bezos, electricity began helping beer makers about a hundred years ago. At that time, there was no power grid. The only way for them to get power was to set up their own generator and become experts in electric power generation.

"The important thing to notice here is that the fact that they generated their own electric power did not make their beer taste better," said Bezos.

We tell ourselves that we're optimizing for scale and efficiency when chasing the latest tech, when in reality, what we're most often doing is best defined as productive procrastination.

Undifferentiated heavy lifting doesn't improve your product. It doesn't make your beer taste better.

Can your monkey juggle fire? If not, stop wasting time and money on pedestals.

This chapter is about not getting ahead of ourselves. First, a few stories about people being happy when their work gets stolen. From there, I'll share a shockingly effective way to launch a product or service, whether it's new or not.

Pirates of the World

In his book *Unlabel*, Marc Ecko tells the story of walking down Tung Choi Street in Hong Kong, an area infamous for selling fakes, with an executive from Timex. He complained to his colleague that Eckō Unlimited was being knocked off and sold illegally.

"Marc, you'll get a lot angrier when you *don't* see any fake Eckō," his colleague responded.

Don't be worried that they might steal from you. Be pissed off that they aren't doing it already.

Paulo Coelho's sold more than 210 million copies of his books. He's a master storyteller, a master marketer, and an active supporter of piracy of his own work.

In 2012, he called on the "pirates of the world" to "unite and pirate everything that he's ever written," teaming up with file-sharing website Pirate Bay to allow users to illegally download every one of his books.[4]

On March 13, 2015, he used his Facebook page to thank a teenager in Delhi for selling illegally printed copies of his book, calling it, "The smallest bookstore in the world." His post has 44.2k likes and 2.7k shares.[5]

"The more often we hear a song on the radio, the keener we are to buy the CD. It's the same with literature. The more people 'pirate' a book, the better. If they like the beginning, they'll buy the whole book the next day," wrote Coelho.

We have a family friend who was working on a secret project. She wouldn't share with us (or anybody else) what it was for fear her idea would be stolen. Three years later, she quietly released a self-published textbook.

Having the idea for an ambitious project like a textbook is easy. Selling it is hard. I know, because I've done it.

I happened to be one of the most well-suited people in the world to help our friend, having earned tens of millions of dollars via a self-published textbook.

Sadly, her project failed. She was so scared of her idea being stolen that I never knew what she was working on and couldn't help until it was too late.

I'll never forget a conversation early on in my business journey. I had started my website and called an old colleague, Carolina, for advice.

To be honest, I don't remember what the idea was. But at one point I remember saying, "Nobody's doing this, so I don't want to share it yet."

She interrupted me and, in her heavy Argentinian accent, said: "Jon, I will stop you. If it is true that nobody is already doing your idea right now, it is because it is a shit idea."

$846,706

Over the course of seven days in 2019, I helped 930 personal trainers generate 4,298 new clients, each paying $197. The system had an 84 percent success rate, and the average trainer got 4.62 clients. In total, in only seven days, these trainers generated $846,706 in profit. (Their only expense was the payment-processing fee.)

I called it the "Founding Client Challenge." It's what I call a *permission launch* and can be applied to any industry. For the sake of our example, here are the steps specific to fitness coaching:

1. You've created a new, sixty-day fitness or nutrition program.
2. You need five founding clients (max) to help test it.
3. You don't have everything figured out yet.
4. You're offering a huge discount.
5. If they complete the steps, they get their money back (so, it's free).
6. It starts on a firm date.

Newness is great for business. It's a damaging admission that can be used to justify a promotion complete with a discount, urgency (time running out), and scarcity (quantity running out). Independent of one another, these elements are effective. Combine all three and you have a great offer.

In some cases, the trainers were new to online fitness training. In other cases, the trainers used this model to run out a new program (or give their existing service a new name) and jump-start their clientele.

To get their founding clients, the trainers reached out to their existing network. Some of them had email lists or social media pages, but many didn't. What they discovered was that they all had a list—friends, family, and former colleagues to whom they could reach out. What I taught them was how to not be weird about it.

In his song "Feel This Moment," the rapper Pitbull shares the secret to effective (and non-awkward) outreach:

> Ask for money and get advice
> Ask for advice, get money twice.[6]

This was their "permission launch" process:
1. Identify the type of person your program can help.
2. Write down the names of fifteen people you're already connected to in that market.
3. Ask them for advice on a new project.

Here's an example outreach message:

Hey [name]!

I'm working on something exciting and I would really benefit from your insight and feedback. Its goal is to help working moms organize their chaotic life a bit better.

I know you're super busy, but is there fifteen to twenty minutes in the coming days we could chat on the phone to learn more about your day-to-day so I can figure out where I'm right (and wrong) with what I'm building?

Once on the phone, at the end of the call, the trainer said that the regular price will be $500 but the price for a "founding client group" is 60 percent off ($197) starting next week. Actually, however, it's free, because when the person completes it, they get their money back. Then they asked if their friend knew anybody who might be interested.

Additionally, they promoted their founding group across their social media platforms or email lists if they had it. Some also sent cold emails directly asking people they knew to participate, though most didn't feel comfortable doing that.

On the final day before the deadline, the trainer sent a "last chance" follow-up reminder to anybody who showed interest.

Before the program began, the coach booked a "checkpoint" call with all participants for day forty-six. On this call, the coach congratulated each client for their progress, painted a picture of what could be achieved over the next three months, and offered to put the $197 toward the next phase of training instead of returning it. Over 85 percent agreed.

———

Getting Jiggy

Showing up to the bar is scary. It takes guts to wear nice clothes and put yourself out there in the hopes that you'll meet someone special.

Standing on the dance floor, nervously shuffling your feet, maintaining eye contact with nobody in particular, and searching for that stupid tiny straw bobbing in your raspberry vodka, hoping it finds your mouth, dammit, wishing somebody would invite you to dance, rarely results in success.

If you want to dance, simply showing up to the bar is not enough. Putting on your cleanest pair of Pumas and standing at the edge of the dance floor is not enough.

Don't ever assume people know you're in business or how to do business with you. In our heads, it's clear. In our world, it's obvious. We've already made the ask. We're at the bar. Of course we want to dance. "Why isn't anybody asking me? Look at my feet; I'm wearing my dancing shoes, for fuck's sake! I have a logo and content. But, but, but there's a link in my bio!"

The problem is that other people don't live in your world. They live in theirs. And they're also standing on the edge of the dance floor wondering why nobody is asking them to get jiggy with it.

In your mind, prettying up your social media profile or iterating on your logo should make it clear that you're in business. But everybody else is doing the same thing. So, while it's clear to you, others don't notice.

If you want something, talk to a human and ask for it.

And, yeah, you'll get rejected sometimes. It'll suck. But the person who gets rejected the most is also the person who is most likely to find a dancing partner. At the end of the day, getting rejected and not asking have the same result. So, here's advice from an awkward white guy who has an uncanny ability to dance the precise opposite of whatever beat is playing: Ask.

—

Permission to Launch

During his rise to power, the Founding Father Benjamin Franklin would ask to borrow books from influential men.

What Franklin correctly identified is that humans have a bias for consistency. A small favor leads to future favors. Here's a passage from his autobiography describing how he turned an enemy into a supporter by borrowing a book:

> Having heard that he had in his library a certain very scarce and curious book, I wrote a note to him, expressing my desire of perusing that book, and requesting he would do me the favor of lending it to me for a few days. He sent it immediately, and I return'd it in about a week with another note, expressing strongly my sense of the favor.
>
> When we next met in the House, he spoke to me (which he had never done before), and with great civility; and he ever after manifested a readiness to serve me on all occasions, so that we became great friends, and our friendship continued to his death.
>
> This is another instance of the truth of an old maxim I had learned, which says, "He that has once done you a kindness will be more ready to do you another, than he whom you yourself have obliged.

Permission launches are a wonderful way to launch any new idea, even for established companies.

In 2022, I was preparing to release a software platform called QuickCoach for fitness and nutrition coaches to build and deliver plans to their clients.

The platform's amazing. The problem? Nobody wants more software. I knew that once people tried it, they'd love it. Getting them to try it was the challenge.

Once we had a working prototype, I made a list of sixty colleagues and asked if they'd do me a favor and chat on the phone. "I'm building something special and it'd be really helpful if I could ask you some questions about how you build and deliver your programs to your clients," I said.

I did forty short calls focused on their process and frustrations with it. At the end, I shared a prepared thirty-second description of what I was building and asked if we could schedule another call for feedback on the prototype after I incorporated what I learned from our conversation.

Thirty-five people were excited for a tour of the prototype a month later. When launch day came, these colleagues felt some ownership of what we created. Many told friends and shared the promotional video—helping it get more than a hundred thousand views in twenty-four hours. The result was five thousand users on day one.

The sooner you sell, the faster you figure out what you actually have. Until you make a sale, everything is a guess. Perhaps educated, but a guess nonetheless. The first step is to make a sale. Build your pedestals later.

Next, two words to become more valued.

CHAPTER 13

Find Your "So That"

A Shelf — Suing Surgeons — Ask, Don't Tell — The Bed of Nails Paradox — "So What?" vs. "So That"

Just doing something doesn't make it valuable. Just being someone doesn't make you valued.

In your own head, the value that you provide is obvious. Less so for others.

How your product or service works doesn't matter. What your thing does doesn't matter. What matters is what somebody wants to become as a result of what you do.

And everybody's wants are different.

—

Think about what your phone does.

You press a button. A signal shoots down FROM FRIGGIN' OUTER SPACE. Your phone catches the signal (somehow) and translates it AT THE FRIGGIN' SPEED OF LIGHT into random facts like who hit the walk-off home run for the Toronto Blue Jays in the 1993 World Series (Touch 'Em All, Joe!) to videos of pandas eating bamboo, which, by the way, are very fun to watch.

Nobody understands how this all happens. We can re-create it. But we don't really get it. It's literally magic.

And still, nobody's excited about their phone bill.

What's exciting is meeting your soulmate on a dating app. What's exciting is making a pregnancy announcement in your family's group chat. What's exciting is showing off on social media the turtle you found at Playa Pátzcuarito, a remote black sand beach in Mexico.

Most people promote what they do as if it's an itemized phone bill:

When you sign up for Jonathan Goodman's Fabulous and Fantabulous Coaching for People Who Want Strong Bodies and Stuff (JGFFCPWWSBS), you get:
- Three calls with me, every two months
- An update to your plan every two weeks
- Access to my private community
- Fitness programming

Now, I know what you're thinking: *Awesome coaching company name and super-sweet acronym, Jon.*

Thank you.

But also, the above list of features isn't very compelling, is it? I bet you glossed over it.

Gigabytes are a feature. Talking to a girl you're into is a benefit. Features are logical; they speak to the head. Benefits are emotional; they speak to the heart. Emotion drives action; logic justifies it. Only discuss features if they're connected to benefits.

These are the ten categories of benefits that drive action.

1. Love
2. Health

3. Security
4. Salvation
5. Self-regard
6. Independence
7. Financial stability
8. Sex / sexual fulfillment
9. Community and peer recognition
10. Beauty / desirability / personal attractiveness[1]

Once I meet my soulmate, I'll get love, we think. *Once I tell my family we're having a baby, I'll improve my self-regard,* we predict. *Once I post about my vacation, I'll gain peer recognition,* we assume. The words we use might differ but the concept remains.

———

Pela Case has sold more than one million compostable phone cases. They cost $55 to $65. That sounds crazy when you consider that a simple search on Amazon results in hundreds of cases that protect a phone just fine selling for $15.

It's not crazy at all when you consider what Pela Case is actually selling. They're selling phone protection, sure, but what they're really selling is self-regard. A phone case is something we interact with every day and something others we interact with see. To somebody concerned about the environment, a cheap plastic case says, "I don't care about the environment," while a Pela Case says, "I'm part of the solution." An extra $40 one time for daily self-regard is a great deal.

Sell people what they want and give them what they need. They *need* your product or service; they *want* the results of it.

First, let's learn how to figure out what matters to others.

Next, the Bed of Nails Paradox of communication.

And finally, I'll equip you with a small word change that makes a big difference in how you're valued by others. Let's dig in.

A Shelf

Let's say you want to drill a hole in your wall. I'm a contractor. You found my phone number online and called me (and probably others), asking for help.

Well, you wouldn't ask me to help because I'm embarrassingly bad with tools. So, let's say you asked my wife, who is very handy around the house. It's not why I married her, but it's a distinct added benefit and I happened to be the one talking to you about the job. That's convoluted. Anyway, we're talking about a hole.

On the phone, I'd ask you why you wanted the hole because there's lots of types of holes we can make.

You might say that you need the hole in order to hang a shelf. I'd ask you what you wanted to put on the shelf.

And maybe you'd tell me that you want to put a picture of your grandfather and his urn on it. You'd say that you loved him as a kid and want to remember him and all the happy memories that you had together.

You don't want a hole. You want to remember your grandfather.

Other contractors could drill you a hole. I'm the only one who knows *why* you want it.

The poet M. Scott Peck wrote, "You cannot truly listen to anyone and do anything else at the same time."

"It's rare to listen to somebody in totality," said Julian Treasure, a sound and communication expert. "Giving somebody your full attention is the greatest gift you can give to another person."

Listen with curiosity. Your intent is to understand, not reply or impress.

Treasure's RASA is a helpful four-step, active-listening framework.[2]

1. Receive

Effective listening means facing the other person and making eye contact. Give that person your full attention.

2. Appreciate

As the other person speaks, show you're paying attention with affirmatory actions and noises. Nod your head, smile, and add little noises like *uh-huh*, *mm*, and *wow* where appropriate.

3. Summarize

Once the other person is done speaking, transition to the next part of the conversation with the word "so" and summarize what was said. "So, what you're saying is that ____."

4. Ask

Avoid closed questions with possible agendas like, "Does this need to be strong enough to hold books?" and instead rely on open-ended questions like, "What are you wanting to put on the shelf?"

———

Suing Surgeons

According to Malcolm Gladwell in his book *Blink*, "People don't sue doctors that they like." Dissatisfaction leading to litigation is never solely the result of bad medical care. It's assumed to be bad medical care because of bad patient care.

Customer satisfaction is the result of three factors:

1. How important they're made to feel
2. If it worked (according to the customer's definition of a good result, not yours)
3. If they felt supported throughout

Surgeons who had never been sued spent, on average, more than three minutes longer with each patient. They were also better listeners, displaying what patients described as more humor and a better tone to the doctor's voice, which demonstrated genuine concern for their welfare. Finally, the surgeons who were never sued were more likely to encourage questions and engage in active listening.

Here's the craziest part to me though. The psychologist Nalini Ambady was able to accurately predict which surgeon got sued without hearing any words. She developed a technique called *thin slicing* that removed high-frequency sounds.[3] All that was left was intonation, pitch, and rhythm.

If a surgeon's voice was judged to be dominant, the odds were better that the surgeon was in the sued group.

If a surgeon's voice was judged to demonstrate warmth, the surgeon tended to be in the non-sued group.

The judges knew nothing about the surgeon's experience, training, or what procedure was performed. They didn't even hear the words that the surgeon said to the patient.

"In the end it comes down to a matter of respect, and the simplest way that respect gets communicated is through tone of voice, and the most corrosive tone of voice that a doctor can assume is a dominant one," wrote Gladwell.

Yes, your expertise matters. So does the quality of your product and service. But how people *feel* they're treated by you matters more.

———

Ask, Don't Tell

Are you breathing fast or slow right now?

Did you think about your breath? If so, consider what just happened to your awareness.

With words on a page, I just changed your physiology. We're not talking. We're not even in the same year, let alone in the same room.

We want to feel like we're in the driver's seat for our lives.

Questions have the power to shift focus while allowing a person to maintain a feeling of autonomy. When you're asking somebody to buy, you're asking them to make a change—maybe a big one, or maybe a small one, but a change nonetheless—and all change involves ambivalence. We don't like to be told what to do.

The Obvious Choice dances with ambivalence. The more autonomy you can give a potential customer, the more likely they'll buy and do what you say.

Consider the difference between these two statements:

"In my mentorship, we help you become one of the most successful people in the industry by showing you what they're doing that you're not."

Versus

"When people ask what my mentorship is about, I respond with this challenging question: Do you ever wonder what the most successful people in this industry know that you don't? Like, what the heck are they doing that you're not?"

Both statements say the same thing. The first is my words. The second invites the receiver to tune into their internal dialogue.

I don't know why people think they're not successful. I can guess, but I don't need to guess. All I need to do is cast light upon the tension that already exists within their mind.

Good questions don't create tension, they illuminate it. You aren't the cause of their pain, but you can be the solution.

Ask, don't tell.

Tension's required for change. Asking for a sale isn't just asking for money, it's also asking the person to change—change in belief systems, consumption habits, or daily patterns.

If you're being told that you're too expensive, odds are you're being lied to.

Money's rarely a real objection. The real objection is most often an unwillingness to change stemming from a lack of tension. Basically, it's not important enough to them right now because you haven't made them aware of how important enough it *should* be for them right now.

—

My background's coaching, but over the past thirteen years I've studied and performed a lot of sales—phone sales, paid advertisements, direct mail, social media, affiliate, email, and everything in between. Our companies have generated millions of dollars in profit from them. And in that time, two things have become clear:

1. Selling is coaching.
2. The best coaching is consultative.

Magic words don't sell. Curious and confident skepticism sells. When we buy, we all want the illusion of autonomy—to feel like we're the boss of ourselves.

Buying your thing must feel like their decision.

—

The Bed of Nails Paradox

The retired basketball player Shaquille O'Neal asked fans to name his new boat in a Facebook post.

"Call it 'Free Throw' so you won't ever sink it," was the top reply, which is hilarious.

Shaq didn't have a well-rounded game. He was one of the worst free throw shooters in history, shooting a career 52.7 percent from the line. It didn't matter. He's in the Hall of Fame because of how dominant he was in the paint.

A famous parlor trick is to lie down on a bed of nails, enjoy the gasps of onlookers who think the nails will pierce your skin, and then bask in applause as you stand up, unscathed.

There's nothing magical about the trick. It simply demonstrates the principles of pressure—the application of force over a particular area.

If you step on a single nail, it goes straight through your foot. Why? Because all the force—your weight—is concentrated on the tiny area of skin that makes contact. A bed of nails, on the other hand, distributes that same amount of force over such a large surface area that the nails don't break the skin.

Powerful communication focuses on a single nail.

More isn't better. Focus on one thing. **Each new element you talk about in your marketing diminishes the power of the others.**

If your nail isn't immediately obvious, create a single-question post-purchase survey:

"I'm curious. What made you want to buy (name of your thing) right now?"

Feedback based on actual purchases immediately at the time of purchase is most accurate. They have to see your question immediately after they buy. Catch them in the heat of the moment.

For example, Girls Gone Strong is a company that sells a certification in post-pregnancy to health professionals. They were pleasantly surprised to discover that a lot of men were buying. So, they asked what was going on in the man's life. Out of everything he could buy, why this and why now?

In almost every case, somebody close to the man (a client, spouse, or family member) got pregnant, which triggered the purchase. GGS then became centered around providing support for loved ones and not about making more money in the industry by being a more credentialed professional.

—

Writing this reminds me of a time when a friend's visit turned into a business consult.

He had been working for a gym for years and finally set up his own youth strength and conditioning facility. It wasn't going well.

I knew he needed his thing—his nail—and asked him to talk me through his client sessions. To my surprise, there wasn't a single treadmill or piece of cardio equipment involved. Here's what he said (paraphrased) when I asked him if this was normal.

These athletes are busy, man. They're kids.

They have school and want to hang out with their friends.

I see them two or three times a week and there's no guarantee they'll do workouts on their own, especially if it's steady-state cardio. Not only that, overuse injuries from long-distance running are a big problem in youth sports.

If we do all the skills and strength work we need at the right pace, the kids will get a cardio-training effect. Everybody knows that, though.

Within eighty-five words, my friend described:

- **The problem.** Kids are busy.
- **The pain.** Kids want to be kids and hang with their friends.
- **The pain for parents (who pay the bills).** Injury avoidance.
- **The solution.** Pacing the workout to get a cardio-training benefit.

His nail—incorporating cardio into the workouts—is one of many things he does. The next action is for him to brand it as his own in two steps:

1. Give it a unique name.
2. Create content highlighting the problems with other workouts and how his proprietary system solves them.

There were four damaging words at the end of his answer. Did you catch them?

"Everybody knows that, though," he said.

My friend passed off his nail as common knowledge. And among his fellow coaches, it is.

Do the parents of youth athletes know, though? I doubt it.

One more example.

Bulletproof Upgraded Coffee claims that their Bulletproof Process removes all mycotoxins—a fungi that likely causes inflammation, fatigue, and possibly cancer.

I'm sure it's true they remove it. But you know what else is true? All commercially imported coffee, in every developed country, has removed the stuff for at least the last forty years.

In their book *Coffee Physiology*, published in 1988 (decades before Bulletproof Upgraded Coffee hit the market), the authors wrote, "Mycotoxins have sometimes been associated with coffee: here again their importance should not be dramatized as they do not present an undue toxicological hazard with the good manufacturing practices normally encountered in coffee production."

Everybody in the coffee industry knew how nasty mycotoxins were. They also knew that their process removed them. The public didn't, though. Bulletproof recognized the marketability of this information asymmetry and made it their nail.

When we're surrounded by people who think like us, it's easy to be tricked into thinking that what we know isn't special. To people like you, it's not. The people buying aren't like you, though. They don't know what you know.

Here, once again, you're too close to your own thing.

"So What?" vs. "So That"

Finally, a small word change that makes a big difference.

The worst thing somebody can think when you're describing what you do is "so what?"

Fortunately, there's an easy trick.

Moving forward, whenever you mention a feature, add a "so that" statement connecting it with a benefit.

A few examples:

- "We offer seven gigabytes of data so that you can post videos of your adventures abroad for your friends at home."
- "We deliver 'fast five' programming to your kids so that they avoid injury, get a great workout, and dominate the playing field."
- "Our blender has a powerful 1,560-watt motor so that you can crush ice and make a delicious and nutritious cold smoothie that your kids will love."

In every case, you've taken a nice-sounding yet relatively common, mundane, and otherwise meaningless feature and presented it as a valuable benefit to a specific person, making the choice of what to buy, well, obvious.

Next up, what to do, because social media is obviously not enough.

CHAPTER 14

Social Media Is Not Enough

*A Better Way — Toys That Do More — The
Four-Stage Content-Creation
Framework — The Quality of the Trade*

F or every eighteen-year-old on social media who thinks they need a big following just to make a few sales, there are a hundred silent business owners quietly earning more.

"The information economy," according to journalist Oliver Burkeman, "is essentially a giant machine for persuading you to make the wrong choices about what to do."[1]

Creating content is an overrated way to build a business.

———

Snoop Dogg and Solo Stove once teamed up on a viral marketing campaign that earned 19.5 billion global media impressions.[2]

In it, Snoop said he was "giving up smoke."[3] The smokeless fire-pit company gained sixty thousand new social media followers.[4] *AdAge* ranked it the eighteenth best advertisement of 2023.[5]

Two months later, Solo Stove's CEO resigned with this statement: "While our unique marketing campaigns raised brand awareness of Solo Stove to an expanded and new audience of consumers, it did not lead to the sales lift that we had planned."

A share doesn't help business if nobody cares about the business.

Improved brand awareness can be beneficial long-term. Just don't depend on content for your short-term success.

Social media's best thought of as a lagging, not leading, indicator of impact. It amplifies what's already there. It's the fuel, not the fire.

I'll say it again: Think of your online platform as a savings account. Make investments when you have extra time and money. It's okay to hope that it kicks off ongoing interest so long as you plan for it to take years to develop into anything meaningful.

By now, you might think that I'm anti–social media. Far from it. Everybody should build their online platform. The way most people do it is burning them out, though. Let's change that. It can be a great use of time.

—

A Better Way

Jeff Steinberg's problem wasn't making sales; it was attracting enough people to sell to.

Once they were in his free, private community, converting them into clients for the Fit Parent Project was straightforward. His problem was that social media wasn't generating interest; nobody was joining his community.

You don't compete with other business owners when you create content. You compete for attention with full-time influencers.

Feeding the machine is exhausting. On top of running a business, it's often too much. If you enjoy content creation, then, obviously, don't stop doing it. Most don't. Most people tell me it's a constant source of anxiety, frustration, and burnout, but they don't know a better way.

If everybody's standing on tiptoes at a parade, nobody has a good view. Don't copy them. Find your own parade or saddle up next to somebody who's already found a good seat.

Instead of trying to attract parents through his own content, Jeff found Mompreneurs with at least ten thousand followers. These women were already selling healthy products at premium prices to Jeff's target market. And people who buy premium health products buy lots.

Rhowena, "Rhow," owned and operated Healing Mama Co. They made pre- and postpartum kits for expectant mothers. Rhow's Instagram page had 22,000 followers.

At the time, an Ultimate Labor & Postpartum Hospital Bag from Healing Mama Co. cost $288.88. Jeff bought one and did a collaborative giveaway with Rhow on Instagram. To enter, people had to join Jeff's Fit Parent Project online community (which is where the winner was announced). More than a hundred people joined.

Most people view social media as a tool for generating attention. And it is. But you've got to be all-in on content creation—a game most business owners I speak to don't want to play.

A better way is to build your account like it's a sales page with updates, case studies, and testimonials. Its job isn't to attract attention, it's to convert attention attracted elsewhere.

Jeff's minimum coaching package costs $2,000. He could run seven promotions with Rhow and get one client to break even.

Within six months of shifting his focus away from the content hamster wheel, his business grew to the point where his wife quit her unfulfilling job and joined him in the business. And Rhowena, she was happy, too. She made a sale.

—

Toys That Do More

Sara Feldstein left her accounting career to design "Toys That Do More" through her company, Barumba Play. Her first ambitious product: a kid's modular play couch.

An inspiring story of resilience and overcoming, Sara got a lot of press and even won Visa's She's Next grant. Not only that, her TikTok content started to get hundreds of thousands of views.

None of these things sold couches.

The major press was good social proof to feature on her website, but it didn't generate customers. The TikTok content, well, it turns out that calling yourself an accountant on TikTok is a discreet way of saying you're a sex worker. So, people on there thought Sara was a prostitute selling play couches that "do more." They were understandably disappointed.

Barumba Play is what I call an avocado business.

> Not yet.
> Not yet.
> Not yet.
> EAT ME NOW!
> Too late.
> —Avocados

Avocados have a short shelf life to be eaten.

A customer doesn't know they exist. Then the customer is shopping for a new home. If you don't catch the customer at that very second and show them how amazing play couches are, you're too late; they're out of space.

Sara's challenge is to insert herself into places where people go when they're ready to buy—knowing that a few days earlier they probably didn't know play couches existed.

She found play couch review articles already ranking in Google. Then, she wrote an addition with Barumba Play, formatted in the style of the page, and emailed it to the blogger. It took ten minutes to create.

"The easier you make it for them, the better chance that they'll say yes," said Sara.

The first review generated $85,000 in net sales. So, she repeated the process with another blog and saw $36,000 from fifty-two sales tracked by a referral code.

"Review articles are at the bottom of the funnel. They're great, but there aren't many of them and not everybody is buying at this moment. Most people still don't know what a play couch even is. So, my next job is finding people higher up in the funnel and educating them," Sara told me.

In *Breakthrough Advertising*, Eugene Schwartz describes five levels of customer awareness:

1. Unaware: They don't know they have a problem.
2. Problem aware: They know they have a problem, but don't know about a solution and aren't looking yet.
3. Solution aware: They've begun exploring fixes but don't know about all the options.
4. Product aware: They know about the options and are actively comparing them.
5. Most aware: They know they want to buy but haven't yet.

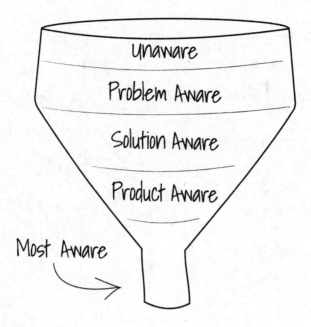

Play couch review blog posts appeal to customers already interested in buying one, because they are actively comparing options. They're product aware.

Next up, she targeted the same sites already sending her sales with articles inserting Barumba Play as a great solution to a problem readers already have. For example, one article is titled "How to Engage Kids on Rainy Days (without TV)."

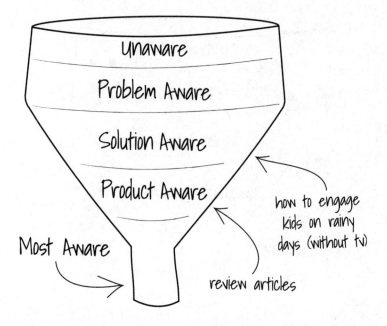

Moving up the funnel one more time, Sara's post-purchase interview provided insight into two problem-aware avatars—people who might not be looking for a solution yet but need one: owners of tiny homes and occupational therapists specializing in supporting autistic children.

She's now googling terms like, "How to Raise a Family in a Tiny Home?" prewriting sections for Barumba Play, and asking that it be added.

Finally, she scrapped the Canadian and American directories of occupational therapists (OTs) and sent cold emails outlining the benefits of play couches for safely engaging autistic children. Then she uploaded those emails to a custom audience and targeted articles to the OTs through paid advertising on social media.

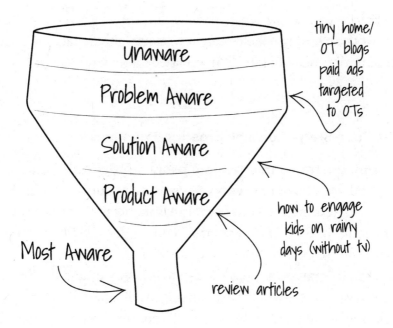

You've gotta meet people where they're at if you want to take them where they need to go. The lower in the funnel you're targeting, the more specific you can be about your thing.

Problem Aware—Call out the problem. Show them that a solution exists.

Solution Aware—Demonstrate how your solution solves the problem better than other options they might be considering.

Product Aware—Compare options. Share reviews and case studies.

Most Aware—Compel them to buy now with any combination of urgency (limited time to buy), scarcity (limited quantity to buy), bonuses, or discounts.

Sara didn't need to get famous as a Mompreneur. She didn't need the ego boost; she wanted to sell couches. Once she made the switch to more purposeful content, it only took a year and a half for her to hit her first million dollars in sales.

Before you do the work, think about the work you are doing. A post to an empty echo chamber on social media takes the same amount of time to create as an update to a review site.

———

The Four-Stage Content-Creation Framework

Getting frustrated that random people in the world aren't impressed by you when you've just started doing something new—something you could never reasonably expect to be good at for a long time, something that you do on the side in between all your other responsibilities—is a mistake.

This, in addition to an addiction to immediacy and the dreaded comparison trap—where we compare our bloopers to others' highlight reels—makes us think that, if we don't get an immediate response to our post on social media, then we're a failure.

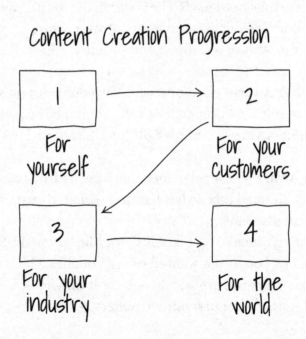

Content Creation Progression

1 — For yourself
2 — For your customers
3 — For your industry
4 — For the world

There's value in content when you're new, and there's value ongoing. The key is to figure out what value you need to get out of it based on your situation at any given time.

First, create content for yourself. Then, for your customers. Next, for your industry. And finally, the world.

Stage 1: Create content for yourself.

Creating content is an overrated way to build a business in the short term but an underrated way to learn. And the best way to learn is to teach.

In 2008, I started my first blog called *The Champion Lifestyle*.[6] Nobody read it.

During that time, I was training ten to twelve clients one-on-one each day, coming home, and reading. Then I'd write short articles about what I'd read and experienced with clients. It accelerated my learning as a trainer and made me a better writer. In the fitness game, we call this "putting in the reps."

Document your journey. Dissociate from the outcome. Produce selfishly for yourself, first, to learn.

Also, thanks, Mom, for the comment on my first blog. It was the only engagement I got for two years.

Stage 2: Create content for your customers.

It's okay to want to impress people as long as you choose the right people to want to impress.

Once you have some customers, make content for them. Nothing you'll say is revolutionary. You've read the same books and watched the same videos as others in your industry. Still, it's helpful. Your people will enjoy getting the information from you.

Focus inward. Aim to help. Be genuine.

Start a newsletter, write a blog, record a podcast, make videos, or publish to social media. It doesn't matter which you choose, so long as the goal is to best serve your existing customers.

In 2010, I wrote a blog for my clients. I'd get asked a question, give an answer, then go home to write an article that I could email to all my clients.

It wasn't that I didn't want to get famous on the internet. I didn't know that it was possible. Optimistic ignorance. Admittedly, the world was different then. Still, the articles weren't trying to impress the world. They were genuinely trying to help the people I was already working with.

Most business owners should stay at stage 2 for their entire career. You'll get many benefits without the drawbacks of impostor syndrome, burnout, and wasted time prevalent in the creator economy.

While it shouldn't be the goal, there's a chance your work will get discovered by people outside your network. Genuine approaches tend to resonate.

A few of my blog posts went viral and got the attention of influential people.

Before long, Livestrong named me one of the forty-five "best trainers you've never heard of." Then *Men's Health* asked me to contribute to a book, and I got offered a writing spot on Arnold Schwarzenegger's blog. At the time, I was a personal trainer working out of a small gym in Toronto.

I learned two things from going viral multiple times:

1. The best content genuinely tries to help a specific person you can name, not impress the world.
2. Getting featured on massive media outlets doesn't lead to business.

None of my newfound attention led to a single training client. Ever. Literally, not one.

There's this wonky misconception that you have to do cool stuff online in order to enable you to do cool stuff in the real world. It's the opposite. Do cool stuff first, then talk about it in a cool way online.

The blog posts that I wrote didn't lead to clients, but they did lead to industry attention. That attention, combined with me being legitimately successful at my job *outside of writing online*, was a potent combination.

Before long, colleagues began asking me what I was doing. So, I started to write about that, too.

Up until this point, following count doesn't matter. If you decide to transition to stage 3, that changes.

Stage 3: Create content for your industry.
Andrew Coates hasn't left his day job. It's where the ideas for his content come from. In addition, he shares his colleagues' work and hosts an interview podcast. In four years, he's earned 150,000 Instagram followers. He further supplements his work by hosting an industry conference.

Andrew's continued investments into his career capital are leading to a bright future. As the podcaster Jordan Harbinger often says, "He's digging the well before he's thirsty."

For two years, from 2011 to 2013, I worked on the Personal Trainer Development Center website (theptdc.com) at night after a full day of clients. I wrote, and I published articles from other industry experts.

Our first product was a crowdsourced ebook called *101 Personal Trainer Mistakes*. I asked colleagues for a contribution, pasted it into a Microsoft Word document, and paid $5 for a cover design. The ebook had three hundred downloads in its first week.

Don't worry about what to sell if you're at stage 3. Your day job should be making you enough money. Instead, focus on building your audience by growing a platform that your colleagues will benefit from.

Then, once you have an audience, ask them what they need, make it, and sell it to them.

By 2015, my website had 4 million visitors per year. From 2011 to 2023, I hosted five conferences, published eleven books, developed six digital products, built a certification course, and developed a software platform. We've served more than 200,000 customers in 120 countries.

Stage 4: Create content for the world.

Elon Musk once tweeted, "For improved quality of sleep, raise head of your bed by about 3" or 5cm and don't eat 3 hours before bedtime."[7]

Musk isn't a sleep expert. His tweet's boring and the advice is basic. Despite that, it got 31,000 shares and 349,000 likes. As a test, I copied his post and tweeted it on my account. It didn't get a single like. The difference is that he's Elon Musk and I'm not.

Thought leadership is primarily about the earned reputation of the person, not the quality of the content.

The truth is that success on social media without success in the real world is exceedingly rare. You ascend to stage 4 by earning a reputation and then you proceed to amplify your impact through content.

If you are at this level, it's helpful to understand why people use social media and how to combine different types of content.

In my book *Viralnomics,* published in 2015, I wrote about how we're all addicted to an invisible drug called IIIAF—we use social media mostly as an act of selective self-representation, as a way to feel like we appear Intelligent, Interesting, Intellectual, Attractive, or Funny.

Whether we actually appear those ways is irrelevant. What matters is that we think we do. Our self-worth isn't impacted by reality. It's impacted by *our* version of reality.

Let me ask you a question: What's a duck's favorite snack? Cheese and quackers.

Whether you think I'm funny doesn't change how I feel about myself. What matters is that I think that you think I am. And that joke's hilarious.

Information gets shared for three reasons:

1. The person sharing wants to become part of a group.
2. The person sharing wants to strengthen their position within a group.
3. The person sharing thinks the material makes them seem funny or sound smart.

Content that best attracts new followers is different from the content that converts them into customers.

Broken down into its simplest parts, thought leaders publish a combination of three types of content:

1. Viral—attracts followers.
2. Value—solves their problems.
3. Depth—creates connection with them.

Purely viral accounts attract the most followers but lack a meaningful ability to sell.

Accounts that only include problem-solving content often lack the size to make an impact.

And if you're only posting personal information, well, you're not creating content, you're sharing stuff about your life with a few friends.

The right ratio of different content types changes. Early on in stage 4, it should be skewed more toward viral. Later, toward value.

You can see examples of viral, value, and depth posts to better understand what the different types of content look like at www.JonathanGoodman.com/Post.

—

The Quality of the Trade

It's too easy to do a bad job these days.

It's too easy to think that you're working, when all you're doing is posting a status update.

It's too easy to think that you're marketing, when all that you're doing is editing a seven-second video with a free app on your phone.

It's too easy to slap together an image, hack together a free website, or bulk send fifty "networking" emails.

Anybody, anywhere, for free, in a day, with a media studio in their pocket, can start a business online and publish content to social media. How wonderful. Truly.

But also, if it's easy for you, it's easy for others.

As a result, there's more noise and less quality than ever. Impressions will continue to get harder to earn and more expensive to buy.

Chasing platforms is exhausting. There might be a best way to take advantage of the algorithm today. But that's going to change tomorrow. Long term, it won't matter.

Trying to win the internet is seductive. In almost every case, people who provide value directly to a much smaller community earn more money. Instead of trying to monetize generalized attention, they monetize the quality of the trade.

Over the course of your career, it's reasonable for your goals to change. That may change how you decide to measure success.

Whether or not you use social media is your decision. If you do use it, define what "making it work" means for you. It was never necessary for success and never will be. It's simply a tool. A potentially useful tool, but just a tool.

Next, the best way to make the most money.

CHAPTER 15

Whales and Minnows

Sexy Pictures — Broke Fighters — The Passive Income Fallacy — Cash for Life — Simple, Not Easy

"Profit and common good are but two sides of the same coin," wrote the Pulitzer Prize–winning author Hernan Diaz in his novel *Trust*.

Make it expensive. Or make it free.

If you want to serve the minnows, you've gotta sell to the whales.

———

All eyes were on me when COVID-19 crushed the fitness industry.

I'd written the literal textbook for online fitness five years earlier as part of the Online Trainer Academy (OTA). Even though we had more than 11,000 alumni by 2021, most of my industry was either unaware or uninterested in remote coaching. Seemingly overnight, everybody was forced online and needed what I had. It was a weird time.

At $1,999, OTA was reassuringly expensive. But my colleagues were struggling. In response to the pandemic, I thought that it would be a good business move to cut costs and drop the price to $799.

Big mistake.

Getting a cheap customer is just as hard as getting a customer who pays you a lot. And when we consider the value cheap customers bring to our businesses, we find that they tend to drain the bottom line and ruin the experience for others.

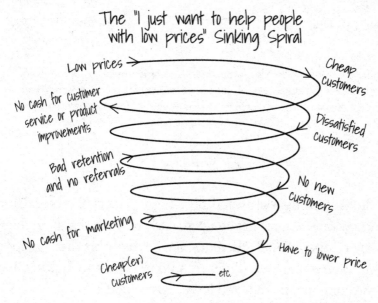

The "I just want to help people with low prices" Sinking Spiral is what happens when you sell your product or service too cheap.

When you don't have enough money to offer a high-quality product and provide great customer service, you end up with dissatisfied customers who don't refer. You're then forced to scramble for new customers by either ramping up paid advertising and/or offering further deals and discounts.

The process spirals downward and puts you out of business.

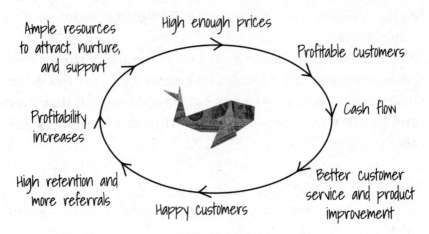

The Whales and Minnows Functional Flywheel

Higher profit leads to better customer service, better product, and, ultimately, more success for your whales. At the same time, it enables you to nurture your minnows, helping and growing them so that when they grow into whales—when they're ready to buy something like your thing—you're the Obvious Choice.

Tesla Motors began by selling a high-priced roadster. Elon Musk knew that he couldn't compete early on with the incumbent automakers' operational efficiency. So, he made his first car cool, different, and expensive. Then he sold it to a few whales. Over time, the company introduced lower-cost models.

Musk knew that it's easier to go downmarket than upmarket. **When your business is new, you lack the necessary scale to make a product that's both good and inexpensive.** So, choose. But remember, you're judged on whether you've solved a person's problem.

It's okay to tell most people to go elsewhere. I forgot that lesson.

More customers and less profit forced me to cut corners. Our customer service, which was previously remarkable, couldn't keep up, the content budget got slashed, the podcast stopped, and new product innovation paused.

Reducing the price so that everybody could afford our product almost bankrupted my company. I turned things around by raising the price by 50 percent. Then, in 2023, I raised it again. The program now costs $1,599.

At the same time, I renewed emphasis on a higher-tier service that costs $10,000-plus for the top 0.01 percent of our industry called the Online Trainer Mentorship and began heavily investing in free content for the 99.99 percent who couldn't yet afford to work with us.

Raising prices turns sinking spirals into functional flywheels.

Whales and minnows is an approach to business that turns "Why should I buy *from you*?" to "Can I please buy from you?" while also making it easy for you to help those who never buy. How ideal.

——

Whales and minnows is also a life philosophy.

Say yes or say no.

Show up or don't show up.

Decide to do the thing or don't do the thing.

Successful people make binary decisions and accept the trade-offs. Unsuccessful people cannot say no to substandard opportunities. They muck about in the middle, afraid to fully commit to a few things, instead opting for the perceived safety of many.

We can't do it all. We can't even do very much. And trying to do it all is a great way to not do any of it well.

"It's not rude to say no to one person if it means you can say yes to more," wrote marketer and author Ryan Holiday. President Harry Truman once wrote a letter in response to a Mr. Taylor in

1954 that said, "Your question will be answered in the book which I am getting ready to publish, as soon as possible."[1] Poetry.

A personal example:

My wife and I went to a John Butler Trio concert. His rendition of "Ocean" damn near took us to a different planet. After the song was done, I looked at Alison and said, "Let's go home."

We were all-in and then we weren't. So, we left the concert early and were in bed by 10:30 p.m., had a good night's sleep, and were fresh for our kids the next morning.

One more example: my family lives abroad every winter.

It's always an adventure. I want to be present. That means not feeling like I need to capture every second with my phone. We hire a local photographer for one afternoon in each location. Twenty great photos are better than thousands of bad ones.

Whales and minnows.

This final chapter is about increasing your perceived value, having fewer customers, charging a lot, and using your extra time and money to help more people.

But the philosophy goes deeper than that.

It's also about the binary decision most people, including me, don't make often enough: show up or don't show up. Both are fine. The middle isn't.

———

Sexy Pictures

Bill's a former marine turned boudoir photographer with long red hair.

Sidney works at the front desk of a hotel making $17 an hour, has three kids, and keeps her hair in a perma-ponytail.

Sidney booked a $350 photo shoot with Bill. After it was done, she bought multiple upgrades including:

- A ten-image photo book for $699.
- One black-and-white print for $599.
- A $300 storage fee, in case she wants to buy more pictures later.

Altogether, she paid close to $2,000 for a few sexy pictures. Which sounds like a crazy purchase for somebody who can barely afford rent.

Here's the review that Sidney left on Bill's services:

I looked at myself completely differently. Just like every one of you, I'm very critical of my body, even after losing twenty pounds last year. It's not perfect, but no one is. . . .

I believe my first words were, "That's not me." I got to see myself in a completely different light. I realized I am beautiful, and any man is lucky to have me.

I felt empowered and ready to conquer the world. I loved myself again!

That last line. That says it all. *Wow.*

Bill did this. Bill made her feel this way. Bill helped Sidney discover who she really was.

His photo sessions include hair and makeup. You're welcome to bring your girlfriends. There's mimosas, chocolate-covered strawberries, and empowering music. Bill's wife hypes you up. And Bill—who I remind you is a former marine with long red hair—puts you at ease by demonstrating the moves himself. Picture that. Or, don't. Yeah, I just pictured it and suggest that you don't picture it. Let's move on.

You're not selling your thing, you're selling what somebody will become as a result of your thing. The more profit that you make, the more resources you have to deliver on your promise.

There's a parable about a master locksmith.

He'd go to a house with a jammed lock. In two minutes, he'd pop off the lock and install a new one. His customers were happy until they saw the bill.

"Two hundred and fifty dollars? For what? It only took you a few minutes. You did it too quickly. How do I know the new one is secure?" they'd say.

On one hand, the customer is right. It was done quickly.

On the other hand, the locksmith trained for decades to master his craft. You're not paying him for his time. You're paying him for his years of experience and expertise.

Most people who share this parable stop there—as a celebration of expertise or to voice frustration about a lack of appreciation of expertise. But it doesn't stop there, does it? Because what people *should* value isn't what they *do* value.

Complaining about a problem, even if the problem is unfair and unjust, doesn't solve the problem and is therefore a waste of energy.

What the locksmith needs to do is pretend to struggle with the lock for twenty-nine minutes and thirty seconds before popping it off. He could sweat, ask for a glass of water, and break a tool or two. People would trust his work more and he could charge twice as much without a fuss. *Glad I called a real expert. It must've been really jammed*, the homeowner would think.

In 2016, the Australian Competition and Consumer Commission (ACCC) fined Reckitt Benckiser $6 million for misleading claims about its Nurofen pain relief products.[2]

Nurofen sold multiple pills tailored to different types of pain—back pain, period pain, migraine pain. The prosecution's argument was that the active ingredient, 342 mg of ibuprofen, was identical.

"While I'm sure the ACCC's chemical facts were accurate, their psychology seems to be wrong," wrote Rory Sutherland in his book *Alchemy*. "Promoting a drug as a cure for a narrowly defined condition, as Nurofen did, also increases placebo power . . . everything the company was doing added to the efficacy of the product."

Call it what you want—deceit, salesmanship, placebo—but sometimes a little benign bullshit is good for everybody.

—

Broke Fighters

Frank Benedetto's key insight was that fighters are broke but fans of fighting aren't.

Instead of relying on his fighters to pay the bills, Frank began viewing them as a marketing expense. In exchange for working with them for free, or almost free, his athletes would share videos of their training on social media and promote Frank as their coach.

Alpha-types love fighting. Those same alpha-types often work high-paying, corporate jobs.

Frank developed a premium coaching service called Train Like a Fighter. He sold it to rich guys who want to brag to their buddies that they train with the same guy as the dude they watch punch and kick and hug (errr, I mean choke) other people on pay-per-view TV.

Sell to the whales, serve the minnows, and use the minnows to attract more whales.

I get pushback whenever I talk about whales and minnows by people who want to build an accessible product or service. They want to help but are going about it all wrong.

A thought experiment:

Let's say that you want to donate toothbrushes to help improve dental hygiene in the developing world. The correct approach isn't to start a toothbrush company that sells to lower-income societies. It's to make a lot of money, buy a lot of toothbrushes, and donate them.

You don't need to make a lot of money from the people you want to help. You need to make a lot of money; then, help.

Within a year and a half, Frank scaled his whales and minnows business to $3 million-plus a year and moved his family from New Jersey to Florida.

———

The Passive Income Fallacy

In 1952, General Mills thought that their Betty Crocker cake mix would be an instant hit. All you needed to do was add water, stir, and bake.

Sales were low. The company couldn't figure out why.

They hired two psychologists who reported that the average American housewife felt guilty because the cake mix was too easy to use. Change the recipe, they suggested. Make it so housewives need to "Just add an egg."

Against all marketing conventional wisdom, General Mills revised the product as suggested, making it less convenient, according to an article in *Psychology Today*.[3] Adding fresh eggs, wrote Susan Marks, the author of *Finding Betty Crocker*, "gave women a sense of creative contribution." The management consultant Robert Fritz later added, "For many people, if success comes too easily, they can't handle it."[4]

Last week I came across a tantalizing tweet that said: "Just woke up to more passive income!" It featured a screenshot of multiple overnight sales of a $27 ebook. Dude is living the dream, right?

I'm not convinced.

You'd have to sell 1,851 items for $27 to make $50,000 more this year (excluding taxes and fees). It would only take twenty-one customers paying you $200 a month to make that same $50,000.

What do you think is easier to find? Twenty-one whales or 1,851 minnows?

Todd Herman, the author of *The Alter Ego Effect*, like me, owns both a coaching business and a Software as a Service (SaaS) company. He posted this to Facebook:

SaaS founder:
—Works eight to twelve hours per day
—Makes $1,000 to $5,000 per month

Coach:
—Works the same or less
—Makes $5,000 to $100,000 per month

Yet people call SaaS revenue "passive."
And the coaching model "unscalable."

Passive income, the way it's promoted most often online, is a fallacy.

Highly profitable, cash-flow businesses are frowned upon. The moment people succeed in one, they often switch to a riskier model where they're forced to work more hours for less money.

Coaching's an example of a business that kicks off a lot of cash. When done right, margins are high and expenses low. It's wonderful. But also, they're active businesses.

Too often, successful coaches get tempted by opportunities promising additional revenue streams like low-cost membership platforms, ebooks, or apps. The thought process is that active businesses won't ever make you rich. That's not true. What's actually happening is a combination of boredom from the day-to-day mundanity and an addiction to frequent sales notifications for small and often insignificant amounts of money.

I have an investment advisor. He's purchased stock on my behalf in Mastercard, McDonald's, and Nvidia among many others. On that same night the guy on Twitter was selling $27 ebooks, people used credit cards, bought happy meals, and purchased microprocessors.

Intuitively, I know my money is working for me overnight. Whenever I check my investment accounts, it's easy to see the numbers go up far more than $27 at a time. But I don't check daily. And I don't get notifications. And there's nothing for me to do. Which is simultaneously the point and the problem. Like baking a Betty Crocker cake, true passive income is so easy that it feels like cheating and that's why people tend to fall prey to the passive income fallacy online, often trading a good business model for a bad one.

In many cases, yes, we should trade our time for money. But our time should cost a lot. If we've found work that's meaningful and fulfilling to us, we should do that work.

—

Cash for Life

I won $4 on my Cash for Life lottery ticket last Christmas. After a sustained gloating period, I wondered: *What does "Cash for Life" really mean?*

Turns out there's two options:

1. $1,000 a week for the rest of your life (cash for life)
2. $1.3 million onetime payment (cash up front)

Which should you take?

I'm thirty-seven years old. Let's assume that I'll live another fifty years.

If I chose cash for life, I'd get 2,600 payments of $1,000 for a total of $2.6 million—double the onetime payment.

What if I took the cash up front?

Investing $1.3 million at a 5 percent annual interest rate becomes $14.9 million in fifty years—5.7 times more than cash for life.

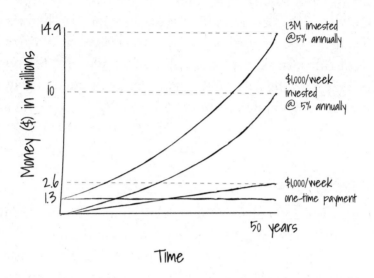

Opting for less cash today but getting it up front and investing it wisely is often a better long-term strategy with both less risk and greater upside than taking smaller amounts ongoing, even if the smaller amounts totalled up equal more starter cash.

Admittedly, I took some liberties with these numbers.

Most startups fail and most influencers crash and burn. But some win big. If you play those games, there's a possibility you'll get a huge payout and end up with more money.

Also, 5 percent compounding year over year doesn't happen. It'll vary. There's luck involved. The rate of return of the market when we start investing impacts lifetime returns measurably.

All of this is kind of the point, though. The future is uncertain. Choosing a business model that kicks off cash today isn't necessarily the best way to optimize wealth, but it's the path with the most reliable odds of achieving "good enough" success.

At a certain point, more money has diminishing returns. If you already have thirty-seven plates of pasta, a thirty-eighth won't make a difference.

But maybe you do have aspirations to get absolutely-positively-stinkin'-rich. That's cool. It's not for me, but not everybody is like me. There are different games to play, and every one of them has different rules, risks, time horizons, and trade-offs. So long as you're okay with the rules of the game you've decided to play, I'm in your corner. Nobody's wrong.

—

Simple, Not Easy

Fix what's inside your fence first, play your own game, remain optimistically ignorant, and become famous to the family.

Stop endlessly searching for the capital-B "Best" way. Instead, find your "g–e" good enough, train the monkey first, and do the thing.

The next time you hear an inspirational story about somebody who overcame against-all-odds, remember that the best lives make for the worst stories. It shouldn't be hard and we shouldn't be surprised when it works. There are no formulaic steps to success. We're all making it up as we go. You can, too.

Admittedly, all of this is hard.

Becoming the Obvious Choice is simple, not easy.

Our brains evolved to collect nuts in a forest, not process a 24/7 information onslaught. It's impossible to keep up.

The modern world's hellbent on convincing us that there's a better way. And perhaps there is. But to that I ask, "If my way is good enough, does a better way matter?"

Like, what are we doing here? And why? To live a better life, right? To show up more for the people we care for. To do good work, but not live to work. To go to bed at night tired, not exhausted. Ready for sleep, but excited to get up and do it again.

———

It's 5:00 a.m. I'm working in the empty lobby of a hotel in the Dominican Republic.

A man stumbled past. Vodka, maybe some rum. He looked at me and said: "That's sad, dude. You're on vacation." At that moment, all I could think about was that I never wanted to once again live a life where I had to go on vacation to *escape*.

"*¿Dónde puedo conseguir un café con azúcar por favor?*"

I asked the lobby attendant in my cave-man Spanish where I can get a coffee. He told me I was too early and would have to wait thirty minutes.

I set out to share a few lessons about success that helped me find my way after I strayed off course. That took me from lost and aimless to being so excited for my work that I was too early for coffee. Lessons that I hope will help you, too.

There's more that I could share. In the future, perhaps I will. But that's enough for now.

It's time for you to find your good, close this book, and execute. Wherever you go, and whatever you do, just remember that the Obvious Choice, after all, is you.

How I Structure My Own Obvious Business

S teve Wozniak, who cofounded Apple with Steve Jobs before famously leaving the company, giving up billions of dollars, once said, "Society tells you that success is getting the most powerful position possible."

Then he added, "But I asked myself: Is that what would make me happiest?"

I love this quote because it highlights the difference between what we're told to want (money/power) versus what many of us actually desire (family/health/happiness/fulfillment/purpose).

—

A friend named David, who wrote a book about weightlifting, was once asked what dead lift was best. "There's no best," he said. "Different shit is different."

Physically, people are different. Financially, people are different, too. There's no "best" way to do this business thing. Your needs and wants and desires are different from mine. Not better or worse; different.

Some people want to own a company, or multiple companies, and understand that with that comes accounting and administration and customer service and a whole lot of other nonsense but in exchange for those annoyances, there's potential for greater financial and reputational rewards.

Others want to work 9–4, go home, and not think about work until the next day. Neither person's wrong.

If somebody has different time horizons, aspirations, family circumstances, and a willingness to work harder—or not work harder—than you, good information for them is bad advice for you.

It's important you figure out what matters to you. Only then can you navigate the noise.

Here's what matters to me.

—

Toronto, Canada (1985–2003)

I had a good upbringing as the youngest of four kids to two loving parents.

My father worked hard as a manager for a logistics company. We didn't see him in the morning because he went to the health club before work.

Fitness doesn't seem like it matters until, one day, it becomes obvious. At seventy-eight, he plays with my kids on the floor while many of his friends are needing assistance.

Still, I missed him at breakfast.

Freedom—to be able to do what I want, with whom I want, when I want—not money—has always been my ultimate goal. Money contributes to freedom, but it's not the only part. And at a certain point, the drive to make more money can detract from freedom.

My goal's to have breakfast and dinner with my family and exercise every day. If that means I make less money or somebody else grows their email list a bit faster than me, that's okay. They've made a choice to work harder and for longer hours than I have. Which is fine.

With that said, I struggle with both envy and jealousy.

I'm aware that some people look at me and envy what I've built. By the same token, I look at others and envy them.

What I've learned is that it's okay to admire what others have without desiring the life they have had to live in order to get it. Defining my true ambition—what *really* matters to me—the stuff that's deeper than dollars—helps me to avoid the recklessness often brought on by comparison.

I'm far from perfect, though. When I fall back into those nasty emotions, I think back to the time when I lived in a hippie sanctuary on a remote island in Thailand, and remember that I kind of like having the freedom to live in weird places like hippie sanctuaries on remote islands in Thailand.

—

Koh Phangan, Thailand (2014)

We lived in a cave. The internet hardly worked.

Our bedroom didn't have a door but it did have plenty of bugs, bats, and frogs. Alison and I slept together on a single gym mat in the sweltering heat for months. Both of us caught a fungus that took years to eliminate.

At that time, the online marketing world was trending toward audio and video media. But there I was, in a cave on an island in paradise with the love of my life, struggling with an internet connection that could barely load a webpage, let alone upload a video to YouTube.

"To invent your own life's meaning is not easy, but it's still allowed, and I think you'll be happier for the trouble," said Bill Watterson, creator of the world-famous comic *Calvin and Hobbes*.[1]

That cave was where I decided what game I wanted to play. In 2014, it was where I decided that my platform was going to be

215

based on writing and not audio or video *because it required less bandwidth.*

In the same talk, Watterson later added:

> We all have different desires and needs, but if we don't dis-
> cover what we want from ourselves and what we stand for,
> we will live passively and unfulfilled.
>
> We define ourselves by our actions. With each decision,
> we tell ourselves and the world who we are. Think about
> what you want out of this life, and recognize that there are
> many kinds of success.

Watterson only ever granted a few public appearances and refused to license his characters—a decision that cost him millions in royalties.

Then, at the height of the comic's popularity, on December 31, 1995, in the final strip, Calvin said, "It's a magical world, Hobbes ol' buddy. . . . Let's go exploring." Calvin and Hobbes then sledded down a hill fresh with snow, a world of possibility ahead, never to be heard from again.

Watterson knew the game, understood the rules, and never lost his way. Then, one day, he decided that he was done. That the job was finished. That he had said what he wanted to say. That even though there was more money to be made, he'd had enough and it was time to move on. How wonderful.

Years later, on May 7, 2017, Alison and I gave birth to our first son: Calvin Goodman.

Working backward from the life I wanted to make my dream a reality has been hard, but I'm happier for the trouble.

———

As expected, the world moved toward audio and video. I saw the trend early on and could have gotten ahead of it. If I had, my platform and community and brand (and income) would likely be much, much larger than it is now.

But, in the ten years that followed, Alison and I traveled for more than 1,600 days, living everywhere from Hawaii to Mexico to Uruguay to Montenegro, Nicaragua, Greece, Dominican Republic, Costa Rica, and more. Where my decision lacked potential financial gain, it made up for many times over in experiential benefit.

Next I needed to define what "enough" meant to me. A Hindu priest in a bathing suit helped me figure that out.

———

Nosara, Costa Rica (2015)

By 2015, business was good but I was working long hours. We were living in Costa Rica, and so was Dandapani, a Hindu priest who now consults with entrepreneurs. He had become a friend.

We met at sunset at Playa Guiones beach. He was knee-deep in the water. Curious where he was living in town, my wife, Alison, asked, "Where are you?"

To which Dandapani replied, "I am here."

That was how our conversation started. That's the kind of guy Dandapani is.

I then asked him the question I'd been struggling with:

"Is there such a thing as too much money? How do I know when I've made enough?"

I'd googled this question multiple times, and the answer never satisfied me. The advice always included some variation of calculating your yearly expenses, assuming an average interest rate, and accumulating enough money in savings where the interest rate on your money paid for your life.

"Enough" isn't a calculation. Humans are too complicated for that.

"If you ever feel like you're being forced into doing something you know in your heart isn't right, that's too much," Dandapani said. "So long as you're doing what you know in your heart is good and you're not tempted to act poorly, make as much money as possible but recognize the line and be careful not to cross it."

Dandapani taught me that "enough" isn't a number. Instead, it's an idea.

He told me that if I wasn't careful, wanting more would trap me in a corner. Wanting more forces people into actions that don't align energetically with what they know is right, tempting them to ignore the people they love; to lie, cheat, and even sometimes steal.

One example: Many of my friends grew their businesses faster than I and made more money by accepting investors and selling equity. Over time, however, I saw their companies and lives become complicated in ways I wouldn't have wanted for myself because they were forced to appease various stakeholders. I've never taken outside investment, and I own 100 percent of my companies. This is a bad decision for growth, but a good decision for me.

——

There's more stories I could tell that helped shape how I think about this stuff but those were a few that stand out in my memory. I hope you now have some insight into what guides me. With that context, here's how I make my money.

——

How I Make My Money

I sell to the whales in order to serve the minnows via four revenue streams:

1. Book sales

2. Coaching for new online trainers
3. High-end mentorship for experienced online trainers
4. B2B SaaS software (QuickCoach.Fit)

Books are on the low end. They aren't free, but I like them because they don't have any expectation of service.

The books are mostly lead generators and lead amplifiers—people find them organically or they find me through social media and aren't ready to participate in a coaching group I offer so buy a book instead.

While my books do make money, business would be fine without them. I write books because I can't not write books. It's a masochistic habit I can't make sense of. This is my twelfth book.

———

Next, I own two coaching groups. Both are for online fitness coaches. They generate a few million dollars in profit each year.

I could help others from other industries but decided to stick with the family I worked hard to become famous to. On one hand, this decision limits my potential growth. On the other hand, it's led to an easier, simpler, and more profitable model.

Some have said that I lack ambition. And perhaps that's true. But I've played the game of sleepless nights worrying about payroll. Of eating cheese and crackers at my desk. Of skipping workouts. And I'm sad to admit that, for years, I was there but not present with my family, preoccupied with "important" business stuff I've long since forgotten. Maybe others have figured out how to have it all: to be ambitious, obsessed with growth; to be physically fit; to be the kind of husband, dad, and friend who's always there—present, energetic, and playful. It's possible I'm simply not as good as others. If that's the case, it is what it is. Two out of three ain't bad.

When you become successful in business, society tries to convince you to scale by going wider, not deeper, as part of an endless quest to make more money. But why? And for what purpose?

If you're an entrepreneur, stop adding complexity into your life that you don't want with time that you don't have for rewards that you don't need.

My first coaching group is the Online Trainer Academy, and it's promoted as a way to get your first clients with online fitness. In it, we help you develop your business structure, programming, packages, and make your first thousand dollars online. But mostly, we help you stop overthinking, get out of your own head, and take action.

The second group is called the Online Trainer Mentorship (OTM). It's promoted to coaches already making at least a thousand dollars online.

OTM helps the top 0.01 percent of coaches scale. What we've found is that most of them got to this point by becoming an expert clinician and winging it on the business end. As a result, they're overwhelmed and lack focus. We give them the systems and accountability to charge more, improve their client service, and prioritize.

Both of these coaching groups have a core operator—an intrapreneur—who runs it as their own thing under my company's umbrella. I built the systems, but both groups operate without my oversight. There are fifteen coaches and salespeople working across both groups.

Compensation for almost everybody is based on either commission or profit sharing. I've found that aligned incentive structures work best to maintain motivation and reduce my own stress. We have almost no overhead that isn't directly related to revenue.

There's no desire to grow either group bigger. For me, for now, this is enough.

OTA and OTM operate at a 65 percent profit margin. The cash they kick off is used to create content for people who can't yet afford to work with us, and generate wealth for my family through long-term investments in the stock market, Bitcoin, and real estate (at a 75:15:10 ratio).

I also founded a software platform called QuickCoach.Fit (QC). It's an app for fitness and nutrition pros to use to build and deliver professional programs to their clients. QuickCoach serves a dual purpose of generating leads for my coaching businesses in addition to being its own profitable business.

Reinvesting cash from the coaching businesses into QC is a risk. While I'm in no rush, it's structured to be sold if/when the time is right. That's the game I'm playing. I knew the rules going in. Time will tell whether the gamble will pay.

That's about it: books, two coaching businesses, a SaaS platform, conventional investing (managed by an advisor), Bitcoin (kept in cold storage long-term), and real estate (managed by a joint venture partner).

My structure is simple and optimized for freedom and profit, not growth.

In the past, I've been more interested in hustling. For this season of my life, with two young boys, I've no desire to get ahead faster. What I'm doing is enough. After all that's happened, I'm happy to report that things are finally going at a good pace.

And with that, it's time for me to go.

A while back, my dad and I booked a celebratory trip to Oaxaca City for the day after this manuscript is due. We leave tomorrow, and I still need to pack.

Time to go exploring!

Jonathan Goodman
Sayulita, Mexico, 2024

ACKNOWLEDGMENTS

I don't know anybody who wakes up at 5:00 a.m. to write or work out that isn't successful. But still, it's hard. And it takes a self-discipline that I lack.

Writing's lonely. Giving up and sleeping in is a constant temptation.

Maybe it's my past career as a personal trainer that taught me the value of external accountability—somebody expecting you to show up and put in the day-to-day work as you grind toward a better you, high-fiving you along the way.

I've been self-employed my entire career. If something gets done, it's because I did it. And if it doesn't get done, it's because I didn't. But I'm human. Most of the time I don't feel like doing the thing I deeply want to do. It's weird. Regardless, with no built-in outside accountability, I have to manufacture it for myself.

Every word of this book was workshopped live on my podcast, also called *The Obvious Choice*. Showing up weekly to present what I'd written forced me to keep plugging away. We even figured out the book's title in an episode and renamed the show soon after to match. (The podcast was originally called *The Goodman Show* . . . because I'm creative like that.)

My first giant thank-you goes to my cohosts on the pod, Ren Jones and Amber Reynolds. This is your book as much as it's my book.

For over one hundred hours, live on the show, you listened and gave feedback on every word in these pages with me. You kept me focused, talked through themes, added stories, and gave me the quiet encouragement I needed to keep going. Thank you. From the bottom of my heart, thank you.

I wrote and edited *The Obvious Choice* for two years in three countries and about a hundred coffee shops. Special mention to the Brentwood branch of the Toronto Public Library, Mugre Animal, La Puesta, and, of course, Tim Hortons, for providing me with plenty of terrible coffee all us Canadians are somehow genetically predisposed to enjoy.

To the medical personnel at Sunnybrook Hospital that treated Alison (I'm looking at you, Dr. E.), thank you.

This is my twelfth book but my first conventionally published one. Self-publishing used to be a point of pride. And perhaps it's good that I had a decade of producing my own books to better appreciate the quality that a world-class team produces.

To my fabulous agent, Jaidree Braddix: I don't know why you came to that conference in Dallas or why you decided to stop me in the hall. But I'm sure as heck glad you did. You're incredible—the partner I didn't know that I needed and now can't imagine working without.

To my editor, Tim Burgard . . . Can I be honest for a moment? I was nervous to work with you. Not you specifically, just editors at major publishing houses in general. I've heard horror stories about them pushing their way on books, taking the author's voice out. My worries were unfounded. You didn't take away my voice; you helped me hone it. Thank you.

To Matt Baugher and the rest of the publishing, sales, and marketing team at HarperCollins Leadership: Thank you for believing in me and supporting me. I appreciate you and I'm grateful for you.

It's amazing to think that my journey started in 2011 in my one-bedroom apartment, at night, after a full day of clients. From the books, to the Online Trainer Academy, Online Trainer Mentorship, QuickCoach, and all the failed projects in between, we made it up as we went. Nobody funded us. Everything we did, we earned the hard way. I couldn't have done it without the PTDC team. In no particular order, thank you, Jason Maxwell, Misty Overstreet, Alina Parades, Josué Cidalgaba, Reynaldo Reyna, Benjamin Garrido, Carmelina Karas, Sven Drumev, Dan Parker, Drea Maxwell, Malcolm McNeill, Alex Harriman, Jon Vlahogiannakos, Christa Baker, Kristine Williams, Allan Misner, Jordan Tuimaualuga, Jonathan Parra, and everybody who has helped us make stuff, say stuff, and build stuff in the past.

Weight lifting is my mental health outlet. It keeps me sane. If you work in fitness, this next thank-you is for you. Prevention is our society's best chance at combating obesity and preventable disease. But it can be a thankless job. And a low-paying job. And a hard job. Still, it's an important job. What you do matters. A special shout-out to a few of the coaches I've hired and gyms I've joined: Dan Trink, Bryan Krahn, Louis Guarino, Buddy Hammon, Collective Fit in Toronto, Nosara Functional Fitness in Costa Rica, F45 Etobicoke Central, Wellness Gym Cabarete in the Dominican Republic, Kilauea CrossFit in Hawaii, Zen Wellness in Montenegro, and Quilombo in Mexico.

Growing up, every adult that I knew was a lawyer, doctor, teacher, dentist, or accountant. That's why, many years ago, I found myself on the phone with Jayson Gaignard, the founder of the Mastermind Talks business community. He asked me why I was interested in joining. "I just need to meet people like me," I told him.

Okay, here comes the big list of names. Of amazing colleagues I admire that have enriched my life since that phone call. Of people that make me feel less alone in this wacky world of entrepreneurship. Thank you to Michel Falcon, Sara Feldstein, Gillian Mandich, Brad Pilon, Tucker Max, Giovanni Marsico, Tony Gareri, Karan Nijhawan, Simon Bowen, Nic Kusmich, Adam Franklin, Joey Coleman, Jim Sheils, Elizabeth Marshall, Samantha Skelly, Jayson Gaddis, Derek Halpern, Derek Coburn,

ACKNOWLEDGMENTS

Curtis Christopherson, Raj Jana, Matthew Bertulli, Sean Platt, Richie Norton, Alex Ikonn, Floyd Marinescu, Gareth Everard, Laura Beauparlant, Brad Mills, Jeremy O'Krafka, Kristi Herold, Todd Herman, Meghan Walker, UJ Ramdas, Dev Basu, Daniel Demsky, Jesse Cole, Danny Iny, James Tonn, Jason Feifer, Charlie Hoehn, Lou Schuler, Gloria Mark, Shane Snow, Alex Hutchinson, Alex Cattoni, Jason Pak, Lauren Pak, Ben Patrick, Sharad Mohan, Stef Joanne, Alicia Streger, Stephanie Estima, Tracey Ivanyshyn, Sally Hogshead, Jen Gottlieb, Chris Winfield, Corey Wert, Louis Grenier, Sam Parr, Kelsey Heenan, Don Saladino, Mike Doehla, Ben Mudge, Spencer Nadolsky, Greg Nuckols, Adam Bornstein, Kate Solovieva, Alex Charfen, Pat Rigsby, Trevor Newell, Roy Morejon, Craig Clemens, Cory Burch, Ryan Moran, Rudy Mawer, Cyrus Gorjipour, Daniel DiPiazza, Billy Murphy, Dave Ruel, Jordan Axani, Matt Christopherson, Jacquie Chapman, Jason Helmes, John Ruhlin, Kevin Darby, Martin Rooney, Nat Eliason, Shane Parrish, Dan Salcumbe, Lori Kennedy, James Dyson, Jeremy Scott, Ryan Holiday, Ben Pakulski, Mike Matthews, Ed Latimore, Molly Galbraith, Chris Cooper, Luka Hocevar, John Franklin, Gareb Shamus, Jason Crowe, Kiera Carter, Dean Somerset, Dustin Maher, Andrew Coates, Brian Pirrip, Rory Sutherland, Jonah Berger, Alex Cartmill, Bret Contreras, Tony Gentilcore, Ryan Lee, Dan Go, Mike Brcic, Michael Easter, Jordan Harbinger, John Berardi, Steve Kamb, and, of course, Dandapani.

Mom, Dad, Lis, Dan, and Dave—thank you. I love you all. Poh Poh, Gung Gung, Trev, and Geoff—from the first moment Alison brought me home to meet you, I've felt loved and included. Thank you.

And finally, to my boys: Calvin and Jaden. This book would've been finished a year earlier if it weren't for you both. I wouldn't have wanted it any other way.

NOTES

Chapter 1

1. Jim Collins, "A Rare Interview with a Reclusive Polymath." *The Tim Ferriss Show* (podcast), episode 361, February 2019. https://www.youtube.com /watch?v=VCN8MQ4NWy8. Transcript here: https://tim.blog/2020 /12/04/jim-collins-returns-transcript/.

Chapter 2

1. The Decision Lab, "Why Do We Prefer Things That We Are Familiar With?" The Decision Lab, no date. https://thedecisionlab.com/biases /mere-exposure-effect#. In 1968, American social psychologist Robert Zajonc found that subjects responded most favorably to foreign prompts they were shown most often.

Chapter 5

1. Jim Cramer, "Exclusive—Jim Cramer Extended Interview Pt 1." *The Daily Show with Jon Stewart*, season 14, episode 36, March 12, 2008. https:// www.cc.com/video/fttmoj/the-daily-show-with-jon-stewart-exclusive -jim-cramer-extended-interview-pt-1.

2. Cheryl Teh, "China Is Tempting Customers with Its Flawless AI Idols— Virtual Influencers Who Don't Gain Weight, Never Age, and Keep Their Computer-Generated Noses Out of Controversy." Yahoo News, August 12, 2021. https://ca.news.yahoo.com/china-tempting-customers-flawless -ai-024059361.html.

3. Thuy Ong, "The Pandemic Isn't a Problem When You're Computer Generated." *Bloomberg*, October 29, 2020. https://www.bloomberg .com/news/features/2020-10-29/lil-miquela-lol-s-seraphine-virtual -influencers-make-more-real-money-than-ever.

4. Robert Thubron, "Deepfake Joe Rogan Video Promoting Testosterone Pills Spreads on TikTok." Techspot, February 14, 2023. https://www .techspot.com/news/97597-deepfake-joe-rogan-video-promoting -testosterone-pills-spreads.html.

5. Private conversation with Adam Bornstein, editorial director for Arnold Schwarzenegger.

6. Complaint in case 1:24-cv-01484, filed 02/24/2024: https://storage .courtlistener.com/recap/gov.uscourts.ilnd.455615/gov.uscourts .ilnd.455615.1.0.pdf. This case was dismissed on April 12, 2024: https:// dockets.justia.com/docket/illinois/ilndce/1:2024cv01484/455615.

7. Joseph Schafer, "Editorial Comment: Treasures in Print and Script." *Wisconsin Magazine of History*, volume 10, number 1, September 1926. http://content.wisconsinhistory.org/cdm/ref/collection/wmh/id/5475.

8. John H. Lienhard, "What People Said About Books in 1498." Paper presented at the Indiana Library Federation Annual Conference, April 7, 1998. https://engines.egr.uh.edu/talks/what-people-said-about -books-1498.

9. Cristina Mutchler, "A Roundup of Foods High in Magnesium." VeryWellHealth, October 23, 2023. https://www.ted.com/talks/dan _gilbert_the_psychology_of_your_future_self.

10. James Manyika, Susan Lund, Michael Chui, Jacques Bughin, Lola Woetzel, Parul Batra, Ryan Ko, and Saurabh Sanghvi, "Jobs Lost, Jobs Gained: What the Future of Work Will Mean for Jobs, Skills, and Wages." McKinsey Global Institute, November 28, 2017. https://www.mckinsey.com /featured-insights/future-of-work/jobs-lost-jobs-gained-what-the-future -of-work-will-mean-for-jobs-skills-and-wages.

Chapter 6

1. "Gnomes," *South Park*, season 2, episode 17, December 16, 1998. https:// www.imdb.com/title/tt0705927/.

2. Jimmy Donaldson (aka MrBeast), tweet on X (formerly Twitter). https://x.com/mrbeast/status/1768431267505213672.

3. Michael F. Stumborg, Timothy D. Blasius, Steven J. Full, Christine A. Hughes, "Goodhart's Law: Recognizing and Mitigating the Manipulation of Measures in Analysis." CNA, September 1, 2022. https://www.cna.org /reports/2022/09/goodharts-law.

4. *The Obvious Choice Podcast*, episode 199. https://www.theptdc.com /articles/create-immeasurable-word-of-mouth.

Chapter 7

1. *The Obvious Choice Podcast*, episode 123. https://open.spotify.com /episode/2Lbz3alW665hLG4TXm8s4N.

2. Jonathan Goodman. "Artificial Intelligence: Redefining the Role of the Personal Trainer." Google Doc. Last updated December 28, 2020. https://docs.google.com/document/d/1JgHJnK_aNmk_Lcsyk9Lf ZZVqX5jOi2J7xd_xY11teYc/edit?usp=sharing.

Chapter 8

1. Simon Sinek, "Together Is Better." Speech to the Royal Society for the Arts (video), no date. https://www.youtube.com/watch?v=AIkfdhGhxDc.
2. Dan Go, tweet explaining the 85% rule. X (formerly Twitter), August 12, 2023. https://x.com/FitFounder/status/1690364931252830208?s=20.
3. Daniel F. Chambliss, "The Mundanity of Excellence: An Ethnographic Report on Stratification and Olympic Swimmers." *Sociological Theory* 7, no. 1 (1989): 70–86. https://doi.org/10.2307/202063.
4. Olivier Poirier-Leroy, "7 Olympic Swimmers on How They Stay Motivated." YourSwimBook, no date. https://www.yourswimlog.com/how-olympic-swimmers-stay-motivated.
5. Steph Smith, "How to Be Great? Just Be Good. Repeatedly." *Steph Smith Blog*, June 12, 2019. https://blog.stephsmith.io/how-to-be-great/.
6. Paul Saffo, "Never Mistake a Clear View for a Short Distance." Bright Sight Speakers, 2014. https://youtu.be/u8NrFDocBFo.
7. Gottfried Paasche, "General von Hammerstein & Hitler: An Exchange." *New York Review*, October 14, 2010. https://www.nybooks.com/articles/2010/10/14/general-von-hammerstein-hitler-exchange/.
8. Quoteresearch, "The Person Who Is Clever and Lazy Qualifies for the Highest Leadership Posts." Quote Investigator, February 28, 2014. https://quoteinvestigator.com/2014/02/28/clever-lazy/.
9. Tim Kreider, "The 'Busy' Trap." *New York Times*, June 30, 2012. https://archive.nytimes.com/opinionator.blogs.nytimes.com/2012/06/30/the-busy-trap/.
10. Andrew Huberman, "Tim Ferriss: How to Learn Better & Create Your Best Future." *Huberman Lab* (podcast), June 2023. https://open.spotify.com/episode/1YMkvaDkN7N7ZwwMpq9kS5.
11. W. Mischel and E. Ebbesen, "Attention in Delay of Gratification." Semantic Scholar, October 1, 1970. https://www.semanticscholar.org/paper/Attention-in-delay-of-gratification.-Mischel-Ebbesen/29346b98f0947a822b8744f4792bcf1a297f01d3.
12. Daniel J. Benjamin, David Laibson, Walter Mischel, Philip K. Peake, Yuichi Shoda, Alexandra Steiny Wellsjo, and Nicole L. Wilson,

"Predicting Mid-Life Capital Formation with Pre-School Delay of Gratification and Life-Course Measures of Self-Regulation." *Journal of Economic Behavior & Organization* 179 (2020): 743–756., ISSN 0167-2681, https://doi.org/10.1016/j.jebo.2019.08.016.

13. Tim Ferriss, "Neil Gaiman." *The Time Ferriss Show* (podcast), episode 366, March 30, 2019. https://tim.blog/2019/03/30/the-tim-ferriss-show-transcripts-neil-gaiman-366/.

14. Vanessa M. Patrick and Henrik Hagtvedt. "'I Don't' Versus 'I Can't': When Empowered Refusal Motivates Goal-Directed Behavior." *Journal of Consumer Research* 39, no. 2 (2012): 371–381. https://doi.org/10.1086/663212.

Chapter 9

1. Laura Stample, "Why This Company Sent Poop to 30,000 People for Black Friday." *Time*, December 15, 2014. https://time.com/3634443/cards-against-humanity-poop-black-friday/.

2. Kickstarter, project page for the Sports Bra, https://www.kickstarter.com/projects/thesportsbrapdx/the-sports-bra-a-womens-sports-bar-and-restaurant.

3. Tom Huddleston Jr., "43-Year-Old's Bar for Women's Sports Brought in $1 Million in 8 Months—This 1 Sentence from Her Business Plan Made It Happen." Make It, October 18, 2023. https://www.cnbc.com/2023/10/18/the-sports-bra-7-word-motto-launched-lucrative-bar-for-womens-sports.html.

4. David Nordquist, "I Lost 40 Pounds for a *Warhammer*-Inspired Movie Role" (video). MiniWarGaming, September 2023. https://youtu.be/h-NOve8bWAo?si=5oEidy_woCSvMkRD.

5. Brendan Maldy, "Ken Griffey Jr. Owns Over 100 Copies of His Rookie Card." *Sports Illustrated*, February 5, 2014. https://www.si.com/extra-mustard/2014/02/05/ken-griffey-jr-rookie-card.

6. Livia Albeck-Ripka, "Baseball Card Sold for $12.6 Million, Breaking Record." *New York Times*, August 28, 2022. https://www.nytimes.com/2022/08/28/us/mickey-mantle-card-auction-baseball.html.

7. Bryan Horling and Matthew Kulick, "Personalized Search for Everyone." *Google Blog*, December 4, 2009. https://googleblog.blogspot.com/2009/12/personalized-search-for-everyone.html.

NOTES

8. Jason Deans, "Google Chief Warns on Social Networking Dangers." *The Guardian*, August 18, 2010. https://www.theguardian.com/media/2010/aug/18/google-facebook.

9. Eli Pariser, "When the Internet Thinks It Knows You." *New York Times*, May 22, 2011. https://www.nytimes.com/2011/05/23/opinion/23pariser.html.

10. "Christina" and Jonathan Goodman, "Overcoming Online Stage Fright." Hot Seat Episode 47, *The Obvious Choice* (podcast), April 2023. https://www.theptdc.com/articles/overcoming-online-stage-fright.

11. Jonathan Goodman, founder, Online Trainer Academy (website). *The Fundamentals of Online Training* (textbook) is available with course. www.theptdc.com/ota.

12. There are many websites that list the commemorative days of the year. For your convenience, here's one: "Days of the Year," https://www.daysoftheyear.com/.

Chapter 10

1. "Herb Kelleher on the Record, Part 2." *Bloomberg*, December 22, 2003. https://www.bloomberg.com/news/articles/2003-12-22/herb-kelleher-on-the-record-part-2.
Herb Kelleher: "We will hire someone with less experience, less education and less expertise, than someone who has more of those things and has a rotten attitude. Because we can train people. We can teach people how to lead. We can teach people how to provide customer service. But we can't change their DNA."

2. Greg Warman, "Design Thinking in Action: Building a Low-Cost Incubator." *ExperiencePoint* (blog), February 16, 2010. https://blog.experiencepoint.com/2010/02/16/design-thinking-in-action-embrace-global/.

3. Technology Exchange Lab, Embrace Infant Warmer (product website). https://techxlab.org/solutions/embrace-infant-warmer.

4. Embrace, Embrace Portable Incubator (product website). https://www.embraceglobal.org/.

5. Colleen Connolly, "How the Coffee Cup Sleeve Was Invented." *Smithsonian Magazine*, August 16, 2013. https://www.smithsonianmag.com/arts-culture/how-the-coffee-cup-sleeve-was-invented-119479/.

6. (Pharma was $630 billion.) Matej Mikulic, "Market Share of Leading 10 National Pharmaceutical Markets Worldwide in 2022." Statista,

December 21, 2023. https://www.statista.com/statistics/245473
/market-share-of-the-leading-10-global-pharmaceutical-markets.
(Vitamins and supplements were $38.9 billion.) NAICS null,
"Vitamin & Supplement Manufacturing in the US—Market Size
(2005–2030)." IBISWorld, February. 26, 2024. https://www.ibisworld
.com/industry-statistics/market-size/vitamin-supplement-manufacturing
-united-states/.
(Fitness and health industry were $30.6 billion.) Christina Gough,
"Revenue of the Fitness, Health and Gym Club Industry in the United
States from 2010 to 2022, with a Forecast for 2023." Statista, December 12,
2023. https://www.statista.com/statistics/605223/us-fitness-health-club
-market-size-2007-2021/.

7. Quoted in: Ken Burns, *Cancer: The Emperor of All Maladies* (documentary film). Premiered on PBS March 30, 2015. https://www.pbs.org/kenburns/cancer-emperor-of-all-maladies/.

8. Quoted in: Candice Millard, *The River of Doubt: Theodore Roosevelt's Darkest Journey* (New York: Knopf Doubleday Publishing Group), December 16, 2009, p. 18.

9. Daniel Ackerman, "Before Face Masks, Americans Went to War against Seat Belts." *Business Insider*, May 26, 2020. https://www.businessinsider.com/when-americans-went-to-war-against-seat-belts-2020-5.

10. Part of this story was told to me in a personal conversation. I filled in the gaps with this interview: Joel Weldon, "Success Comes in Cans Not in Cannots." *I Love Marketing* (with Joe Polish and Dean Jackson, podcast), episode 170, no date. https://ilovemarketing.com/joelweldon-success-comes-in-cans-not-in-cannots/.

11. *The Obvious Choice Podcast*, episode 217. https://www.theptdc.com/articles/217-help-people-understand-what-you-do.

12. Harley Finkelstein and David Segal, "How Issy Sharp Built the Four Seasons and Transformed the Hospitality Industry Forever (Part 1)." *Big Shot* (podcast), June 2023. https://open.spotify.com/episode/6N8BihqbTnuQ16OAHND2IU?si=069ceed3babc44b3.

13. *The Obvious Choice Podcast*, episode 205. https://www.theptdc.com/articles/become-a-master-tribe-builder.

14. Personal conversation with Mike Doehla.

15. Kelly Groehler and Grace Rose, "Self Esteem Brands Acquires Digital Nutrition Coaching Brand Stronger U." Business Wire, June 8, 2021.

https://www.businesswire.com/news/home/20210608005694/en/Self-Esteem-Brands-Acquires-Digital-Nutrition-Coaching-Brand-Stronger-U.

16. Clifford S. Asness, "Pulling the Goalie: Hockey and Investment Implications." SSN, March 8, 2018. https://papers.ssrn.com/sol3/papers.cfm?abstract_id=3132563.

17. Alex Kirshner, "How the Eagles Conned the Patriots on Nick Foles' Trick-Play Touchdown Catch." SBNation, February 5, 2018. https://www.sbnation.com/nfl/2018/2/5/16972668/super-bowl-52-nick-foles-touchdown-catch.

18. Combination of Dandapani's book and *The Obvious Choice Podcast*, episode 193. https://www.theptdc.com/articles/finding-fulfillment-according-to-a-hindu-priest.

19. Personal conversation with Shane Snow.

Chapter 11

1. Sapphire Studies (website). https://www.sapphirestudies.com Story, told to me via a private conversation.

2. Quoted in: Robert Greene, *The 48 Laws of Power* (New York: Viking Penguin Books, 1998), p. 100. Originally published in French in 1688: Jean de La Bruyére, *Les Caractères ou les Mœurs de ce siècle*.

3. Dale Carnegie, *How to Win Friends and Influence People* (New York: Pocket Books, 1958), p. 15.

4. Rory Sutherland, "Perspective Is Everything." TED-Ed (speech), 2014. https://www.youtube.com/watch?v=uXKilrFGd2U.

5. Galata Cafe (website). https://www.galatacafe.ca/.

6. *The Obvious Choice Podcast*, episode 238. https://www.theptdc.com/articles/investing-in-local-relationships.

7. *The Obvious Choice Podcast*, episode 211. https://www.theptdc.com/articles/design-charity-events-that-benefit-your-community-business.

8. Jen Gottlieb describes her fifteen-minute routine to build relationships: https://www.instagram.com/reel/CtjVlRFMySq/.

Chapter 12

1. Astro Teller, "Tackle the Monkey First." Google X, The Moonshot Factory, December 7, 2016. https://blog.x.company/tackle-the-monkey-first-90fd6223e04d.

2. Derek Thompson, "Google X and the Science of Radical Technology." *The Atlantic*, November 2017. https://www.theatlantic.com/magazine/archive/2017/11/x-google-moonshot-factory/540648/.

3. Jeff Bezos, "Jeff Bezos at Startup School 08." Startupschool, 2008. https://youtu.be/6nKfFHuouzA.

4. Alison Flood, "Paul Coelho Calls on Readers to Pirate Books." *The Guardian*, February 1, 2012. https://www.theguardian.com/books/2012/feb/01/paulo-coelho-readers-pirate-books.

5. Paul Coelho is honored by book "pirating": https://www.facebook.com/paulocoelho/photos/a.241365541210.177295.11777366210/10153068240216211.

6. Pitbull, lyrics to "Feel This Moment," *Global Warming*, February 4, 2013. https://genius.com/Pitbull-feel-this-moment-lyrics.

Chapter 13

1. From Jeffrey Lant, *How to Make a Whole Lot More Than $1,000,000 Writing, Commissioning, Publishing and Selling "How To" Information* (Cambridge, MA: Jeffrey Lant Associates, 1993).

2. Julian Treasure, online course: "How to Speak so People Want to Listen." https://www.juliantreasure.com/5-part-video-series/rasa.

3. N. Ambady and R. Rosenthal, "Thin Slices of Expressive Behavior as Predictors of Interpersonal Consequences: A Meta-Analysis." Semantic Scholar, 1992. https://www.semanticscholar.org/paper/Thin-slices-of-expressive-behavior-as-predictors-of-Ambady-Rosenthal/df0c9ca7be20eee0b7c5436332c20dcf46b2109d7.

Chapter 14

1. Oliver Burkeman, *Four Thousand Weeks: Time Management for Mortals* (New York: Farrar, Straus and Giroux, 2021).

2. Belle Communication, "Think BIG: Snoop's Solo Stove Campaign, Food and Bev Trends + Nostalgia in Marketing." Belle Communication, December 19, 2023. https://www.linkedin.com/pulse/think-big-snoops-solo-stove-campaign-food-bev-trends-jrxbc.

3. Here's the link to Snoop Dogg's tweet on X (formerly Twitter): https://x.com/SnoopDogg/status/1725196796618817785.

4. Bart Schaneman, "How Solo Stove Landed the Snoop Collaboration." The Daily, December 11, 2023. https://thedaily.outdoorretailer.com/news/brands-and-retailers/how-solo-stove-landed-the-snoop-collaboration/.

5. Tim Nudd, "The 40 Best Ads of 2023." *AdAge*, December 7, 2023. https://adage.com/article/year-review/best-ads-commercials-creative-marketing-2023-year-review/2532851.

6. The original blog is offline but has been archived and can be found here: https://web.archive.org/web/20130401061737/http://championlifestyle.blogspot.com/.

7. Here's the link to Elon Musk's tweet on X (formerly Twitter): https://x.com/elonmusk/status/1546518224887496705.

Chapter 15

1. The Truman letter was purchased by Ryan Holiday, and it's on display in his office.

2. Australian Competition & Consumer Commission, "Federal Court Orders $6 Million Penalty for Nurofen Specific Pain Products." ACCC, December 16, 2016. https://www.accc.gov.au/media-release/full-federal-court-orders-6-million-penalty-for-nurofen-specific-pain-products.

3. Drew Boyd, "A Creativity Lesson from Betty Crocker." *Psychology Today*, January 19, 2014. https://www.psychologytoday.com/ca/blog/inside-the-box/201401/creativity-lesson-betty-crocker.

4. Robert Fritz, "Just Add an Egg." Robert Fritz, Inc., February 1, 2015. https://www.robertfritz.com/wp/just-add-an-egg/.

Afterword

1. Bill Watterson, "Some Thoughts on the Real World by One Who Glimpsed It and Fled." Commencement speech, Kenyon College, May 20, 1990. https://web.mit.edu/jmorzins/www/C-H-speech.html.

SOURCES AND SUGGESTED REFERENCES

Brunson, Russell. *Expert Secrets: The Underground Playbook for Converting Your Online Visitors into Lifelong Customers.* Carlsbad, CA: Hay House Inc., 2022.

Burkeman, Oliver. *Four Thousand Weeks: Time Management for Mortals.* New York: Picador Paper, 2023.

Carnegie, Dale. *How to Win Friends and Influence People.* New York: Pocket Books, 1998.

Cialdini, Robert. *Influence: The Psychology of Persuasion (New and Expanded).* Homebush West, NSW, Australia: Generic Publications, 1905.

Clarke, R. J., and R. Macrae, eds. *Coffee Physiology.* New York: Springer Publishing, 1988.

Clear, James. *Atomic Habits: An Easy & Proven Way to Build Good Habits & Break Bad Ones.* New York: Avery Publishing, 2018.

Dandapani. *The Power of Unwavering Focus.* New York: Portfolio, 2022

Diaz, Hernan. *Trust.* New York: Penguin Publishing, 2023.

Ecko, Marc. *Unlabel: Selling You Without Selling Out.* New York: Atria Books, 2013.

Franklin, Benjamin. *The Autobiography of Benjamin Franklin: The Original 1793 Edition.* Independently published, 2022.

Gerber, Michael. *The E-Myth Revisited: Why Most Small Businesses Don't Work and What to Do About It.* New York: HarperBusiness, 2004.

Ghafari, Luay. *Seed to Table: A Seasonal Guide to Organically Growing, Cooking, and Preserving Food at Home.* Miami: Yellow Pear Press, 2023.

Gladwell, Malcolm. *Blink: The Power of Thinking Without Thinking.* New York: Back Bay Books, 2007.

Goodman, Jonathan, *Viralnomics: How to Get People to Want to Talk About You.* Charleston, SC: CreateSpace Independent Publishing, 2015.

Harari, Yuval Noah. *21 Lessons for the 21st Century.* New York: Random House, 2018.

Hogshead, Sally. *How the World Sees You: Discover Your Highest Value Through the Science of Fascination.* New York: HarperBusiness, 2014.

Kirkpatrick, David. *The Facebook Effect: The Inside Story of the Company That Is Connecting the World.* New York: Simon & Schuster, 2010.

Lant, Jeffrey. *How to Make a Whole Lot More Than $1,000,000 Writing, Commissioning, Publishing, and Selling "How To" Information.* Cambridge, MA: Jeffrey Lant Associates, 1993.

Marks, Susan. *Finding Betty Crocker: The Secret of America's First Lady of Food.* Minneapolis: University of Minnesota Press, 2007.

Michalowicz, Michael. *The Pumpkin Plan: A Simple Strategy to Grow a Remarkable Business in Any Field.* New York: Portfolio, 2012.

Millard, Candice. *The River of Doubt: Theodore Roosevelt's Darkest Journey.* New York: Anchor Books, 2006.

Pariser, Eli. *The Filter Bubble: How the New Personalized Web Is Changing What We Read and How We Think.* New York: Penguin Books, 2014.

Ries, Al, and Jack Trout. *The 22 Immutable Laws of Marketing: Violate Them at Your Own Risk.* New York: HarperBusiness, 1994.

Schwartz, Eugene, *Breakthrough Advertising.* Boone, IA: Bottom Line Books, 2004.

Zevin, Gabrielle. *The Storied Life of A. J. Fikry: A Novel.* New York: Algonquin Books, 2014.

ABOUT THE AUTHOR

JONATHAN GOODMAN is the creator of the Personal Trainer Development Center and host of the popular *Obvious Choice* podcast, a top show for coaches, entrepreneurs, and small business owners. Jon's been featured in most major business and fitness publications, including *Men's Health*, *Forbes*, *Entrepreneur*, *Robb Report*, and many more. More than two hundred thousand coaches and small business owners in more than 120 countries have purchased business development materials from him. Originally from Toronto, Jon spends his winters exploring the world with his wife and two young sons.